中国思想文化术语多语种对外翻译
标准化建设项目成果
CHINESE THINKING AND CULTURE
MULTILINGUAL TERMINOLOGY DATABASE

中华源·河南故事
CHINESE CIVILIZATION
Stories from Henan

农业

FEEDING THE PEOPLE — AGRICULTURE

主编　张改平
EDITOR-IN-CHIEF: ZHANG GAIPING

河南大学出版社
HENAN UNIVERSITY PRESS
·郑州·

图书在版编目（CIP）数据

中华源·河南故事. 农业 / 张改平主编. —郑州：河南大学出版社，2019.3

ISBN 978-7-5649-2662-5

Ⅰ. ①中… Ⅱ. ①张… Ⅲ. ①地方文化－河南－通俗读物②农业史－河南－通俗读物 Ⅳ. ①G127.61-49 ②F329.61-49

中国版本图书馆CIP数据核字（2019）第047032号

责任编辑	时 娇 姜 畅
责任校对	毛晓旭
封面设计	翟淼淼
出版发行	河南大学出版社
	地址：郑州市郑东新区商务外环中华大厦2401号　邮编：450046
	电话：0371-86059701（营销部）　0371-86059753（大众读物分公司）
	网址：hupress.henu.edu.cn
排　版	河南博雅彩印有限公司
印　刷	河南博雅彩印有限公司
版　次	2020年5月第1版
印　次	2020年5月第1次印刷
开　本	710 mm×1010 mm　1/16
印　张	11.75
字　数	163千
定　价	61.00元

版权所有，侵权必究

本书如有印装质量问题，请与河南大学出版社营销部联系调换。

"中华源·河南故事"系列丛书编委会

顾　　问　　黄友义　杨　平　范大祺
名誉主任　　穆为民　何金平
主　　任　　付　静
副 主 任　　陈志伟　刁玉华　李向前　李　镇　梁留科
　　　　　　刘金锋　孔留安　史永庆　许二平　万正峰
　　　　　　杨建伟　杨玮斌　王建修　王自文　张改平
　　　　　　张松文　赵卫东

主　　编　　付　静
执行主编　　杨玮斌
编　　委　　陈　玮　丁　锐　高　阳　徐恒振

中华源·河南故事·农业

主　　编　　张改平
副 主 编　　张　莉　李喜芬（英文）
中文撰稿　　张　莉　屠　克　李永红
英文译者　　李喜芬　张俊杰　陈　洁　马孝幸

The Editorial Committee
Chinese Civilization Stories from Henan

Consultants	Huang Youyi Yang Ping Fan Daqi
Honorary Directors	Mu Weimin He Jinping
Director	Fu Jing
Deputy Directors	Chen Zhiwei Diao Yuhua Li Xiangqian Li Zhen
	Liang Liuke Liu Jinfeng Kong Liu'an Shi Yongqing
	Xu Erping Wan Zhengfeng Yang Jianwei
	Yang Weibin Wang Jianxiu Wang Ziwen
	Zhang Gaiping Zhang Songwen Zhao Weidong

Chief Editor	Fu Jing
Executive Chief Editor	Yang Weibin
Editors	Chen Wei Ding Rui Gao Yang Xu Hengzhen

Chinese Civilization Stories from Henan Feeding the People — Agriculture

Editor-in-Chief	Zhang Gaiping
Associate Editors-in-Chief	Zhang Li Li Xifen (English Text)
Writers	Zhang Li Tu Ke Li Yonghong
Translators	Li Xifen Zhang Junjie Chen Jie
	Ma Xiaoxing

总 序

中国是世界四大文明古国之一，也是世界上唯一的古代文明传统未曾中断的国家。河南省地处中国中东部，是中华文明和中华民族的重要发祥地，在中国五千年的文明史上，河南作为国家政治、经济、文化的中心就长达三千多年。从某种意义上讲，一部河南史就是半部中国史。这里是中华人文始祖黄帝的故乡，是古丝绸之路的东方起点，是少林功夫和陈氏太极的发源地，这里创建了中国历史上最早的都城，镌刻了中国最古老的文字，诞生了中国最初的商业文明。

伴随着新时代的荣光，河南经济社会发展迅速，人民生活水平显著提升，这是自力更生、艰苦奋斗的历史结果，也是对外开放带来的益处。河南经济社会的发展、人民生活方式的改变都植根于深层次的文化积淀。为了让世界更多地了解河南，让河南更好地走向世界，2018年以来，河南省外事办认真研析了这片古老土地上的历史文化资源和时代风貌，组织各领域权威专家学者，编译了"中华源·河南故事"中外文系列丛书，选取少林功夫、太极拳、中医、汉字、文物、焦裕禄、红旗渠、丝绸之路、古都、农业、手工艺等多个主题，力图以故事的方式向世界展现一个立体、全面、真实的河南。

当今世界，人类文明无论在物质还是精神方面都取得了巨大进步，特别是物质的极大丰富是古代世界完全不能想象的。同时，当代人类也面临着许多突出的难题，比如，贫富差距持续扩大，物欲追求奢华无度，个人主义恶性膨胀，社会诚信不断消减，伦理道德每况愈下，人与自然关系日趋紧张，等等。要解决这些难题，不仅需要运用人类今天发现和发展的智慧和力量，而且需要运用人类历史上积累和储存的智慧和力量。河南历史文化底蕴深厚、包容性强，在今天仍极具现实意义。中原文化蕴含的思想智慧有助于修身养性，推动人类社会进步发展，焦裕禄精神、红旗渠精神所体现的为民爱民、艰苦奋斗的价值取向是构建人类命运共同体的力量源泉。我们期待与读者们一起从河南故事中汲取更多的智慧和力量，共同创造更加美好的未来。

Series Foreword

China is one of the four ancient civilizations in the world, and is also the only country in the world where the ancient civilization has not been interrupted. Located in east-central China, Henan Province is an important cradle for the Chinese nation and the Chinese civilization. In the course of the five thousand years of Chinese history, for more than three thousand years it served as the political, economic and cultural center of the country and therefore, as generally accepted, represents half of the history of China. Henan is the native place of Yellow Emperor, the cradle of Chinese culture, the starting point of the ancient Silk Road in the east, and the birthplace of Shaolin Kungfu and Chen-style Taijiquan—typical examples of the world-renowned Chinese martial arts. It was here that the earliest capital city in China was founded, the oldest Chinese characters engraved, and the earliest commerce took shape.

In the new era, Henan has witnessed rapid growth in its economy and remarkable improvement of people's living conditions, owing to the national reform and opening-up policy and unremitting endeavoring of the people. Modern economic achievements and social development as well as the changes of way of life could be traced back to its traditional values and cultural heritages. To enable people from other countries to understand Henan, and let the province integrate more efficiently into the world development, the Foreign Affairs Office of the People's Government of Henan Province, has organized teams of authoritative experts and scholars in relevant fields to compile this *Chinese Civilization: Stories from Henan* in Chinese and other foreign languages since 2018, by crystallizing the excellence of traditions and outstanding features of modern development. The book series include *Shaolin Kungfu, Taijiquan, Traditional Chinese Medicine, Chinese Characters, Cultural Heritage, A Model Official — Jiao Yulu, Man-made River — Hongqiqu Canal, the Silk*

Road, *Ancient Chinese Capitals*, *Handicraft* and *Feeding the People — Agriculture*, etc, attempting to present a panoramic picture of the province.

In today's world, human civilization has made great progress in both material accumulation and cultural and ethical advancement, and the great abundance of materials today, especially, is beyond the imagination of the ancient people. At the same time, however, modern people are also confronted with a lot of problems, such as the widening gap between the rich and the poor, the indulgence in pursuit of luxury and extravagance, the undesirable extension of individualism, the decline of social integrity, and the increasing tension between man and nature. To solve these problems, we need to draw on the wisdom and powers developed today as well as those accumulated in the past. Henan is endowed with a rich historical and cultural heritage characterized by its inclusiveness, and such a heritage remains significant today. The intelligence and wisdom in Henan culture are conducive to self-cultivation and to the promotion of social development. The spirit of serving the people and relentless struggle, as embodied in *Jiao Yulu* and *Hongqiqu Canal*, provides source of strength for building a community with a shared future for mankind. It is our hope that, wisdom and strength from Henan stories, could lead us to a shared brilliant future.

前 言

提到河南,就离不开"农耕"二字。黄河流域是中华农耕文明的发源地,河南因大部分地区位于黄河以南,故名"河南"。河南地处九州之中,故有"中州"之称;河南横跨中国中部黄淮大平原,又有"中原"之谓。

数千年来,这一地区的政治安危关乎天下兴亡,经济起伏关乎国力强弱,文化盛衰关乎民族荣辱,在中国历史进程中发挥着无可比拟的作用。古代的中国以农开元,以农立国,以农为基。农业的起源、农业技术的发明、农业理念的成熟,无不与河南密切相关。河南是农业大省,河南农业发展史可以被看作中国农业发展的缩影。长期以来河南农业在其发展过程中积淀了丰富的农耕文化。

河南早在裴李岗文化时期已经开始种植粟、稻谷等谷物,西周时期农作物得到广泛种植,汉代已有"五谷"之说,魏晋南北朝时期已经掌握了保墒防旱和耕、耙、糖、压、锄的精耕细作技术。农具的发明和使用,提高了农业生产力。上古时期的耒耜、商代的青铜工具、春秋战国时期的铁制农具、秦汉时期的耧车、唐代的曲辕犁的发明与使用,在中国农业发展史上都具有重要的里程碑意义。先进的水利工程和灌溉设施推动了农业进步。大禹"尽力乎沟洫",春秋时期西门豹治邺,孙叔敖在固始修建期思陂,汉代兴修鸿隙陂、六门陂,都极大地改善了当时的农业生产条件。先进的农业思想成为农业发展的重要推动力之一。以《四民月令》《齐民要术》《四时纂要》《耒耜经》《农桑辑要》等为代表的古代农学著述,有的诞生在河南,有的直接涉及以河南为中心的黄河中下游农业，至今仍闪烁着智慧的光芒。发达的农耕文明成就了河南"天下粮仓"的美誉，"中原熟，天下足"成为代代相传的佳话。河南龙山文化遗址处处都有藏粮的窖穴。隋唐六大官仓中，河南占其五，其中洛阳的含嘉仓堪称"中国古代第一粮仓"。

现如今，河南依然演绎着"天下粮仓"的传奇。2014年5月9日习近平总书记走进一片高标准粮田，看麦穗灌浆，问农田建设。他说："河南粮食播种面积在全国是第二，小麦是第一，占全国小麦面积1/4，把河南粮食、小麦抓在手里，全国粮食丰收就有了基础。这是河南的贡献，对国家粮食安全的贡献，也是奉献。"

自古以来，河南不仅生产粮食，还生产思想，生产文化。农耕文明是人类历史上第一种文明形态，原始农业和原始畜牧业、古人类的定居生活等的发展，使人类从食物的采集者变为食物的生产者，这是第一次生产力的飞跃，而这种文化的发展所产生的道德伦理、文化思想为中国物质文明和精神文明建设打下了坚实的基础。千百年来，农耕文化特有的应时、取宜、守则、和谐理念不断得以提炼，并形成中国的哲学精神和传统的文化核心价值观。河南堪称"中国历史自然博物馆"，有数不清的神话传说、农业民谚都诞生在这块土地，也因此孕育和产生了众多的思想学说，不但老庄哲学是典型的中原文化的代表，儒学、墨学等亦属中原文化或其派生文化，汉代经学、魏晋玄学、宋明理学与佛教文化等，都在中原文化中孕育而生。各种思想交相辉映，积淀升华，铸就了中国传统文化的灵魂，深刻影响着中国民族精神的形成。

Preface

The mention of Henan is inseparable from "agriculture". The middle and lower reaches of the Yellow River is the birthplace of Chinese farming civilization. Since most of its areas locates at the south of the Yellow River, it is called "He-Nan" (South of the River). Ancient China was divided into nine prefectures with Henan right at the centre, therefore the province of Henan is also named "Zhongzhou" (The Central State), or referred to as "Zhongyuan" (The Central Plains) with its location across Huanghuai Plain in central China.

For thousands of years, the political stability of this region is related to peace and security of the country, the ups and downs of the economy is vital for the national strength, and the prosperity and decline of culture relates to the state honor, which plays an unparalleled role in the course of Chinese history. Ancient China was founded by farming and built on agriculture. The origin of agriculture, the invention of agricultural technology and the maturity of agricultural concept are closely related to Henan. The development history of Henan agriculture can be regarded as a microcosm of agricultural development in China because Henan is an important province of agriculture with a magnificent, long history of rich farming culture.

Henan began to grow millet, rice and other cereals in the early period of Peiligang Culture, and to plant crops widely in the Western Zhou Dynasty. "Wugu" (five grains—broomcorn millet, millet, bean, wheat and rice) were recorded in the Han Dynasty. The intensive and meticulous farming based on ploughing, hoeing and leveling the land was very popular in the period of the Wei-Jin, Southern & Northern dynasties, which had improved the productivity of agriculture with the invention and use of farm tools. Leisi in ancient times, bronze tools in the Shang Dynasty, iron farming tools in Spring and Autumn Period, Louche (an animal-drawn seed plough) in Qin and Han dynasties, and

Quyuan plow (a curved iron plough) in Tang Dynasty, are all of great significance in the development of agriculture. Obviously, the invention and innovation of farm tools is of vital importance in the history of agricultural development in China. In addition, advanced water conservancy projects and irrigation systems also accelerate agricultural development, for instance, Yu's (also known as Yu the Great) devotion to fight floods in ancient time, Ximen Bao's water diversion structures and Sunshu Ao's construction of Qisi Bei Water Conservancy Project in Spring and Autumn Period, Hongxibei Irrigation Structure and Liumenbei Irrigation System in the Han Dynasty. What's more, agricultural thoughts become an impetus to the development of agriculture. The ancient agronomic works such as *Simin Yueling* (*Monthly Agricultural Activities*), *Qimin Yaoshu* (*Arts for the People*), *Sishi Zuanyao* (*Outline of the Four Seasons*), *Leisi Jing* (*One Kind of Farm Tools*) and *Nongsang Jiyao* (*Fundamentals of Agriculture and Sericulture*) directly involved in agricultural activities in the middle and lower reaches of the Yellow River with Henan as the center, are still of significance. The development of farming civilization has won Henan a reputation as "The Country's Granary". Accordingly, "Crops ripen in the central plains; no one will starve in the world" becomes a much-told story from generation to generation. Barn cellars were everywhere in Longshan Culture sites, Henan Province. Henan had five of the six official warehouses in Sui and Tang dynasties, of which Hanjia Granary in Luoyang was the biggest one in ancient China.

Today, Henan is still known as China's granary. On May 9, 2014, when checking the growth of wheat in a high standard cropland in his inspection tour in Henan Province, President Xi Jinping emphasizes, "Henan's grain sowing acreage is the second in our country, and that of wheat is the first, accounting for a quarter of the total areas in China. Therefore, Henan's grain, especially wheat harvest will lay a foundation for a good harvest year in our country. This is Henan's contribution to national food security."

Since ancient times, Henan has produced not only grains, but also thoughts and cultures. Farming civilization is the first form of civilization in human history. With the development of primitive farming and stockbreeding, the ancient men settled down, became food producers rather than hunter-gatherers, which is the first leap forward in productivity. The moral ethics and culture produced in the process of farming have laid a solid foundation for both the traditional material development and cultural-ethical progress in Chinese nation. For thousands of years, the unique concept of farming culture to be seasonable, appropriate, regulation and harmonious has been compressed into the philosophical and spiritual core of Chinese. Henan is seen as a "museum of Chinese natural history" with numerous myths, legends and agricultural proverbs, which gives birth to various concepts. The philosophy of world-renowned great thinkers Laozi and Zhuangzi is a typical culture of Zhongyuan Culture. Confucianism, Mohism and so on also belong to Zhongyuan Culture or its derivation. In a sense, Zhongyuan Culture also incubates the Confucian classics of the Han Dynasty, the metaphysics of the Wei and Jin dynasties, the Neo-Confucianism of Song and Ming dynasties, Buddhist culture and so on. All these have exerted influences on each other, playing an important role in shaping Chinese traditional culture, and the ethos of Chinese people. The different areas, various ethnic groups, historical inheritance and local folklores of farming civilization not only endow the important features of Chinese culture, but also explain why the Chinese culture continues to flourish.

目录   Contents

第一章 远古曙光——河南原始农业   001
  一、一场伟大的农业革命从这里开始   002
  二、走向成熟的原始农业   008
  三、到处都是粮仓   014
  四、与农业活动息息相关   020
  五、《夏小正》——中国现存最早的农事历书   026

Chapter I Primitive Farming   001
  I. The Initiation of Farming   003
  II. Mature Primitive Farming   007
  III. Ample Granaries in Ancient Times   013
  IV. Artifacts of Farming   019
  V. *Xia Xiao Zheng*: the Earliest Extant Chinese Calendar   025

第二章 孜孜以求——河南传统农业   031
  一、青铜农具的发轫   032
  二、甲骨上的商代农业   034
  三、《诗经》与周代农业   038
  四、铁器、牛耕、水利与农家   042
  五、二十四节气   046
  六、汉代农耕"纪录片"——精美的汉画像砖石   054
  七、中国古代农业百科全书《齐民要术》   060

八、隋唐宋农业大发展 062

九、重视技术、多熟种植——元明清时期的河南农业 066

十、农业生产实践中的"三才思想" 070

Chapter II Traditional Agriculture 031

    I. The Origin of Bronze Farming Tools 033

    II. Agriculture of Shang Dynasty Recorded in Oracle Bones 035

    III. *Shi Jing* (*The Book of Songs*) and Agriculture in the Zhou Dynasty 039

    IV. Ironware, Cattle Farming , Water Conservancy and Agriculturist 043

    V. The Twenty-four Solar Terms 047

    VI. Exquisite Brick and Stone Portraits in the Han Dynasty 053

    VII. Ancient Chinese Agricultural Encyclopedia *Qimin Yaoshu* 057

    VIII. The Great Development of Agriculture in the Sui, Tang and Song Dynasties 061

    IX. Henan Agriculture in the Yuan, Ming and Qing Dynasties 065

    X. The "Idea of Three Vitals" in Agricultural Production Practice 069

第三章 质的飞越——河南现代农业 075

一、中国人的"大粮仓" 076

二、中国人的"大厨房" 078

三、中国人的"大餐桌" 080

四、河南乡村在振兴 084

五、美丽河南在行动　　　　　　　　　　　　　　　090
　　六、打赢脱贫攻坚战　　　　　　　　　　　　　　094
　　七、河南农业走向世界　　　　　　　　　　　　　104

Chapter III Modern Agriculture　　　　　　　　　075
　　I. China's "Granary"　　　　　　　　　　　　　　077
　　II. China's "Kitchen"　　　　　　　　　　　　　　079
　　III. China's "Dinner Table"　　　　　　　　　　　081
　　IV. The Rural Vitalization in Henan　　　　　　　083
　　V. The Construction of a Beautiful Henan　　　　087
　　VI. Win the Critical Battle Against Poverty　　　091
　　VII. Going to the World of Henan Agriculture　　103

第四章 农业神话——远古深处的人文觉醒　　　　　109
　　一、燧人氏教人取火　　　　　　　　　　　　　　110
　　二、伏羲氏教人结网捕鱼　　　　　　　　　　　　112
　　三、炎帝教人耕作　　　　　　　　　　　　　　　116
　　四、黄帝制定历法　　　　　　　　　　　　　　　120
　　五、嫘祖教人养蚕　　　　　　　　　　　　　　　124
　　六、后稷教人辨识五谷　　　　　　　　　　　　　126
　　七、大禹疏导治水　　　　　　　　　　　　　　　128
　　八、酿酒始祖杜康　　　　　　　　　　　　　　　132

九、后羿射日助人抗旱　　　　　　　　　　　　　　136

Chapter IV　Agricultural Myths　　　　　　　　　　109
　　I. Suiren Teaching People to Make Fire　　　　　　111
　　II. Fuxi Teaching People to Net Fish　　　　　　　113
　　III. Yan Emperor Teaching People to Plant Grains　　117
　　IV. Yellow Emperor Establishing Chinese Calendar　　119
　　V. Leizu Teaching People to Raise Silkworm　　　　123
　　VI. Houji Teaching People to Identify Five Grains　　127
　　VII. Yu the Great Taming Rivers　　　　　　　　　129
　　VIII. Du Kang — Father of Wine Making　　　　　　133
　　IX. Houyi Shooting Down the Suns to Help People Combat Droughts　135

第五章　农业习俗——诗化的农耕文明　　　　　　　141
　　一、立春日，打耕牛　　　　　　　　　　　　　　142
　　二、二月二，龙抬头　　　　　　　　　　　　　　144
　　三、三月三，上巳节　　　　　　　　　　　　　　146
　　四、五月初五端午节　　　　　　　　　　　　　　146
　　五、六月初一过小年　　　　　　　　　　　　　　146
　　六、七月七，乞巧节　　　　　　　　　　　　　　150
　　七、七月十五中元节　　　　　　　　　　　　　　152
　　八、十二月初八腊八节　　　　　　　　　　　　　152

九、农谚 154

Chapter V Agricultural Customs 141
    I. Beginning of Spring 143
    II. Eryueer Festival (Longtaitou Festival) 143
    III. Sanyuesan Festival (Shangsi Festival) 145
    IV. Dragon Boat Festival 147
    V. The Little Lunar New Year 147
    VI. Qixi Festival (Double-Seventh Day) 149
    VII. Zhongyuan Festival 149
    VIII. Laba Festival 151
    IX. Agricultural Proverbs 153

附录 中国历史年代简表 162

Appendix A Brief Chronology of Chinese History 162

第一章

远古曙光——河南原始农业

Chapter I

Primitive Farming

农业的出现，无疑是人类历史由蒙昧走向文明的伟大革命。原始农业是农业的第一个历史形态，它基本上是与考古学上的新石器时代相始终。生产工具以石质为主。从世界范围来看，两河流域文明是基于麦作农业，中美洲文明是基于玉米的种植，华夏文明则是基于粟作农业与稻作农业。大约在距今12 000年时，中国原始农业已经发端。从新石器时代开始，中国已经进入了完全意义上的农业阶段。漫长而悠久的农业发展历史形成了具有中国特色的农业文化。

一、一场伟大的农业革命从这里开始

河南有广阔的平原，河流众多，气候温暖且日照长，是宜农的宝地。1977年4月的一天，在新郑裴李岗村西的岗地上，村民们正在平整土地。一位叫李铁旦的青年农民挥舞着手中的铁锹干得正起劲，突然铁锹撞到了什么，发出刺耳的声响，把原本没有心理准备的他吓了一跳。他赶忙放下铁锹，用手扒开周围的泥土一探究竟。渐渐地一块鞋底状的石板出现在眼前。这块石板大约70厘米长，30厘米宽，板下有四个小腿。围观的村民谁也说不清这东西是干什么用的。此前，听县文化馆的人说这一带有文物，会不会这就是文物呢？想到这儿，李铁旦加快了刨挖的速度。不久，他居然又在石板的旁边挖出了一个石棒和一些已经石化的零碎骨头。他让人找来一个麻袋，然后把这些石器装进麻袋里，准备送到县文化馆去。当他肩扛着几十斤重的麻袋急匆匆赶往县城时，无论如何也不会想到，自己肩膀上扛着的这块石板将带出中国20世纪考古界的一个重大发现，它的出现把中国农业文明的历史向前推进了一千多年，自己祖祖辈辈居住的这个小村庄也会因它的出现而闻名于世。

裴李岗遗址的神来之物——石磨盘和石磨棒，与石斧、石铲、石镰一道，构成了裴李岗文化极富特色的工具组合，这一先进生产力要素的出土，将中国的农业史提前至8 000年前。

The advent of agriculture is undoubtedly a great revolution in human history from barbarism into civilization. Primitive farming is the first historical form of agriculture, which is basically consistent with the Neolithic Age in archaeology. The tools of production are mainly made of stone. Worldwide, the ancient Mesopotamian civilization was based on wheat farming, Central American civilization on corn cultivation, and Chinese civilization on millet and rice cultivation. Approximately 12,000 years ago, China began its primitive farming. China has entered the stage of agriculture in a complete sense since the Neolithic Age. The long history of agricultural development has formed the agricultural culture with Chinese characteristics.

I. The Initiation of Farming

Henan is a fertile land for agriculture, with a vast plain, numerous rivers, warm climate and long-time sunshine. One day in April 1977, the villagers were leveling land on the west side of Peiligang village in the county of Xinzheng. Li Tiedan, a young farmer, was working hard with a spade in hand. Suddenly, a sharp noise from the spade startled him back. He dropped the spade, removed the soil with hands, and explored carefully. That was a slate, about 70 cm long and 30 cm wide, with four legs under it. No one in the crowd could tell what this was for. However, villagers once heard from the functionaries of the Cultural Center in the county that there are cultural relics around this area. Can this be a relic of ancient times? At the thought, Li Tiedan quickened his work. It was not long before he dug up a stone roller and some pieces of fossilized bone next to the slate. He put them in a sack, hurried to the Cultural Center. He would never have thought that the slate on his shoulder would lead to a very important discovery in Chinese archaeology world in the 20th century and this small village, where his family has been living for generations, will be also famous due to this discovery.

Sure enough, the Peiligang Culture was found right there. The stone roller and quern from the Peiligang site, together with the stone axe, stone spade, and stone sickle, constitute a unique tool set of Peiligang Culture. The unearthed tools of production brought China's agricultural history forward to 8,000 years ago.

Archaeologists have found the same remains from more than 100 sites in

河南新郑裴李岗遗址出土的石磨盘和石磨棒
Stone roller and quern unearthed from Peiligang village, Xinzheng City, Henan Province

　　考古学家们在河南的许多地方先后发现同样遗存100多处，大面积发掘或试掘的有裴李岗、舞阳贾湖等30余处。这些重大的发现使裴李岗文化的面貌不断清晰和突出。8 000年前，在那个远古时代，当地球上绝大部分区域还处在人兽杂处、茹毛饮血的蛮荒时期，裴李岗文化时期的先民们已经开始过上较为安稳的定居生活，并形成氏族村落。一个个村落，坐落在临水的台地或平原的高地上，放眼望去，四周长满野生的谷物。先民们住在半地穴式的茅草屋里，用石头和骨料制作生产用的石器和生活用的骨器。在长期采集野生谷物的实践中，他们逐渐懂得用谷物成熟的种子，在温暖的季节撒在松软潮湿的土地上，可以发芽生长再结出谷子，从而学会了种植谷物——粟。在河南贾湖遗址，还发现了距今8 000年的栽培稻遗存。裴李岗人磨制了坚硬的石斧用以伐木，再用火烧掉覆盖在地上的荒草，然后用磨制的石铲掘地翻土后进行种植。农作物产量与翻松土壤和翻土深浅程度有直接关系，所以，懂得翻松土壤是原始农业一项重要的技术进步。粟和稻在田野里完成自然的生长期后结出穗子，先民们就用磨制的石镰收割。这些石镰制作得工整精美，令人叹为观止。它们都呈拱背凹弧形，刃部被磨成锯齿状，柄部有上下两个缺口，专为绑缚木柄而制。收割的穗子和石磨盘、石磨棒放在一起。

many parts of Henan. Large areas of excavations or trial excavations have been done in 30 more other places including Peiligang and Jiahu. These important discoveries make Peiligang Culture clear and prominent. In ancient times when man and beasts pitted against each other in a savage way on most parts of the earth 8,000 years ago, the ancestors in the period of Peiligang Culture began to live in a more secure, settled way of life, and gradually formed a clan village. Surrounded by wild grains, villages perched on waterfront terraces or on the high ground of the plain. Ancient ancestors in Henan lived in semi-underground thatched huts like caves, made stone tools for production and bone implements for living. In the long-term practice of collecting wild grains, they gradually learned to plant grains by sowing ripe seeds in soft wet soil during the warm seasons, which would make seeds germinate, grow and bear millet. The remains of cultivated rice 8,000 years ago were also found in Jiahu site, Henan Province. In addition, Peiligang people ground hard stone axes for logging, burned grass in the ground, dug the earth with stone spades and planted seeds. Crop yield is directly related to soil loosening and the depth of loosening. Therefore, soil loosening is an important technological advance in the primitive farming. Ancient ancestors in Henan harvested millet and rice with stone sickles which are ingeniously designed. What made them most impressive are the arched back, the concave arc, the serrated blade, and the two upper and lower gaps for securing a wood handle. The harvested grains were placed with the stone rollers and stone querns. The stone quern was made by a slab of sandstone with four legs under it. Its back was polished and its surface was cut like freckles to increase the friction. Ears of millet or rice were put on a big stone quern and crushed with a stone roller for seeds.

  The significance of stone roller and quern is that they create a new era of agricultural development, which shows that people have a stronger ability to accept the gifts of nature. Although they were gradually replaced by more advanced grain processing tools—mortar and pestle in the late Neolithic Age, the initial significance and enlightenment of stone roller and quern can never be overestimated. Ancient ancestors in Henan started agriculture about 8,000 years ago. They opened up fields to grow millet and rice suitable for human as the main source of food, which laid the earliest foundation for the development of human civilization.

河南新郑裴李岗遗址出土的石铲、石斧和石镰
Stone spades, stone axes and stone sickles unearthed from Peiligang village, Xinzheng City, Henan Province

石磨盘是用整块沙石岩琢磨而成，底部的四条腿与磨盘浑然一体，盘的背面做磨光处理，正面人为凿出坑坑洼洼的斑点，以增加摩擦力。先民们将穗子放在磨盘上用石磨棒碾压脱壳取米。

石磨盘和石磨棒的意义在于它创造了一个时代，一个农业发展的新时代，昭示着人们对于大自然的赐予有了更强的接受能力。尽管在新石器时代后期，石磨盘和石磨棒逐渐为更先进的粮食加工工具杵臼所取代，但它的启迪和发端意义是永远无可取代的。河南人的祖先，在距今约8 000年开启了农业时代，选择适宜人类食用的粟、稻类植物的种子进行垦荒播种，使之成为人类食物的主要来源，用勤劳的双手为人类走向文明奠定了最早的基石。

关于新石器时代早期的河南农耕文明，许多史书都有记载。从前，人们只会采集野生植物的果实和根块食用，炎帝教人种植谷物，被天下人称作神农氏。炎帝在农业上创造了许多业绩，史书上说，他教人们砍削树木做木制的耒耜，用以垦荒种地；他教人们烧制陶器，用来煮饭；

Farming civilization of Henan in the early Neolithic Age has been recorded in many historical books. The primitive people could only collect the fruits and roots of wild plants to eat. Then, the Yan Emperor taught people to grow grain, and was accordingly called Shennong (God of Agriculture). In the era of the Yan Emperor, many achievements had been made in agriculture. According to historical records, he taught people to make wooden Leisi (the early plough) for cultivation, to fire clay pots for cooking, to weave clothes for sheltering people from the shame of nudity and the bitter cold of winter and to understand the properties of hundred herbs for treating diseases with herbal medicine. Thus, the Yan Emperor was deified as the god of the sun, agriculture and medicine in many ancient books. Obviously, he embodied the above achievements which were created by the forefathers in Henan. He chose a site in today's Huaiyang District, Zhoukou, Henan, as the capital. Thereafter, the ancient country founded by people whose surname was Jiang in his clan was mostly in Henan Province. Undoubtedly, the early time of the Yan Emperor's era coincided with the period of Peiligang Culture.

II. Mature Primitive Farming

Yangshao Culture appeared about 7,000 to 5,000 years ago. It was so called because it was first found in Yangshao village, Mianchi County, Henan Province. With wide distribution, long history, rich connotation and profound influence, Yangshao Culture can be regarded as the best in all kinds of Neolithic culture in China. The settlement in Peiligang Culture is the product of farming civilization, which in turn promotes the stability and development of a settled way of farming life. Therefore, there were more than 800 village sites of Yangshao Culture. The period of Yangshao Culture was a period which experienced a transition from matriarchal society to patriarchal society, and also from "primitive farming" to "mature agriculture".

During the period of Yangshao Culture, hamlets and villages scattered here and there. People lived in peace, working from dawn to dusk. Yangshao Culture is at the stage of hoeing agriculture, lasting for more than 2,000 years. As mentioned above, in the period of Peiligang Culture, there were mainly single

他创立了纺织手工业，使人们免除裸体之羞、冬寒之苦；他了解百草的药性，从而发明了用草药治病的医术，等等。很多古籍将炎帝神化，说他是太阳神、农业神和医药神。今人都已十分理解炎帝的上述功绩均为先民所创立，炎帝的形象是群体形象。炎帝定都在今天的河南淮阳，炎帝一族的姜姓所建的古国大都在河南境内。炎帝时代的前期与裴李岗文化时期相吻合，这一点毋庸置疑。

二、走向成熟的原始农业

仰韶文化时期大约在距今7 000至5 000年之间，因最早在河南渑池仰韶村发现而得名。仰韶文化分布广泛，延续久长，内涵丰富，影响深远，在中国所有的新石器文化种类中堪称佼佼者。裴李岗文化时期出现的定居村落是农耕文明的产物，反过来又促进农耕生活的稳定与发展，所以，仰韶文化时期的村落遗址就有800多处。仰韶文化是母系氏族向父系氏族过渡时期的文化，也是中国"原始农业"走向"成熟农业"的时代。

进入仰韶文化时期，大小村庄星罗棋布，人们日出而作，日落而息，平静地生活着。仰韶文化处于原始的锄耕农业阶段，这个时期很长，有2 000多年，农业一直处在发展过程中。裴李岗时期的石器工具主要是石斧、石铲和石镰，种类单一。到仰韶文化时期，村落大增，人口大增，耕地需求量也大幅增加。开荒用的石斧首先接受了技术革新，出现了宽刃的、窄刃的、单面刃的、双面刃的、扁平的、弧形的，各种各样，种类齐全，上面还都钻了孔，便于固定，也便于携带。有研究者好奇石斧的砍伐功能，尝试做了试验，结果只用了10分钟，一棵碗口粗的树就被砍断了。但是革新者仍不满意，又进一步发明了省力好用的砍挖工具石锛，可以深翻土地的石耜和割穗用的石刀。仰韶文化早期，人们在农闲的时候还得狩猎和捕鱼，以弥补农业的不足。到了中晚期情况

kind of stone axes, spades and sickles. By the time of Yangshao Culture, with the greatly increased number of villages and population, the demand for cropland was soaring. Thus, the technological innovations brought about all kinds of stone axes. Some researchers were curious about the efficacy of stone axes and tried to do experiments. As a result, it took only 10 minutes to chop down a tree of 10 cm in diameter. Even so, the innovators were never satisfied and further invented stone adze for chopping, which was easy to use and saved effort. They also invented stone spade for turning over soil, and stone knife for harvesting grains. In the early period of Yangshao Culture, villagers had to hunt and fish at slack season to make up for the inadequacy of agricultural produce. At its middle and late stages, the situation was different. The number of tools exponentially increased due to constant innovation. In terms of agricultural knowledge, a wealth of experience was accumulated from thousands of years of labour. And separate, small patrilineal families appeared, with robust men as the main force in farming. What's more, agriculture based on millet entered the stage of "irrigation with implements". That is to say, hand-made utensils, mostly pitcher with small mouth and pointed base, were used to draw water directly from rivers, puddles or wells for agricultural irrigation. This is a major leap forward in agricultural irrigation, surely of epoch-making significance, and accordingly "irrigation with implements" further strengthened the settled way of farming life.

At that time, people in Henan planted at least three kinds of food crops — millet, rice and sorghum. Millet and sorghum are drought-tolerant crops, while rice prefers warm, rainy climate. Grains can be grown in light of different local conditions, and different cropland has also been expanded accordingly. In the middle and late stages of Yangshao Culture, people did not have to go hunting or fishing since there was a surplus of grains, which were usually stored in two ways. A pottery pot was an ideal vessel for grain storage, which is moisture-proof, rat-proof, permeable to air, and easy to access and use. Even now, pottery pots for grain storage are popular with housewives. Another way was to build large barn cellars. The sides of the cellar were smeared with white paste or baked to prevent against moisture.

With the development of agriculture, every family could afford to raise livestock. The captive breeding produced a large amount of manure which in turn

河南南阳淅川马山根遗址出土的磨制石器：斧、锛、铲、刀、球等
Stone axe, stone adze, stone spade, stone knife and stone ball unearthed from Mashangen site, Nanyang City, Henan Province

就不一样了：工具不断改进，数量在原先的基础上成倍地增加；农业知识方面，数千年的劳动积累下丰富的经验；家庭结构方面，出现了父系个体小家庭，身强力壮的男子成了农业的主力军。而且，这个时期，粟作农业跨入"器灌"农业阶段。"器灌"，顾名思义，是使用人工制造的器物，多是小口尖底瓶，用人力从江河、水坑或水井中直接取水，从事农业灌溉。这是农业灌溉中的一次重大飞跃，具有划时代意义。"器灌"农业的产生，进一步巩固了农耕定居生活。

那时，河南的先民们至少会种三种粮食作物，即粟、水稻和高粱。粟和高粱都是耐旱的作物，水稻则喜温暖多雨的气候。种哪种粮食可以因地制宜地选择，耕地种类也随之扩大。仰韶文化中晚期，人们不再像以前那样需要靠狩猎和捕鱼弥补生活的不足，因为粮食出现了剩余。人们通常用两种方法贮存粮食。陶瓮是贮存粮食的理想器皿，防潮，透

fertilized crops to boost yields. This was one of the factors which contributed to the rapid development of agriculture in the period of Yangshao Culture. Scattered bones of domestic animals such as cattle, chicken and pigs were found in almost every site of Yangshao Culture. The pig bones were the most probably because the ancestors knew that pigs grow fast, and they are gentle, prolific, and easy to feed. They preferred its tender meat, delicious taste and manure for farming. As a matter of fact, ceramic pigs, the earliest Chinese art works, have been unearthed in the sites of Peiligang Culture. According to *Shuowen Jiezi* (*Analytical Dictionary of Characters*), the earliest Chinese dictionary, the character "home" is illustrated as "a pig under a house". Does this mean that each family raised pigs? The ancestors may have a sense of food security when they raised pigs in their thatched huts. Raising pigs is also a symbol of settling down.

During the period of Yangshao Culture, the clan society in Henan area was a unified one of the Yan Emperor tribe (or the Yan Emperor clan) and the Yellow Emperor tribe (or the Yellow Emperor clan), but mainly dominated by the latter. According to *Shi Ji* (*Records of the Historian*), the Yellow Emperor, also known as Xuanyuan Yellow Emperor, came to power eight generations later than the Yan Emperor. It is evident that neither Yan Emperor nor Yellow Emperor was a specific name but the titles of two different tribal leaders. The Yellow Emperor established the Youxiong Kingdom with its capital in Xinzheng, Henan Province. Even now, there are numerous legends about the Yellow Emperor and relics related to him in Xinzheng. The Yellow Emperor clan lived in the Central China for more than 2,500 years, with their footprints all over Henan Province. The Yellow Emperor mined copper in Jingshan Mountain, Lingbao County, Henan Province. Pieces of smelted copper were found in the remains of late Yangshao Culture. Unquestionably, copper smelting was such a major technological invention that it had spurred the rapid development of social productivity, and pushed China into the Chalcolithic Age. The Yellow Emperor's achievements in Henan are recorded in many well-known Chinese historical books such as *Shi Ji* (*Records of the Historian*), *Shuowen Jiezi* (*Analytical Dictionary of Characters*), *Han Shu* (*History of the Han Dynasty*), etc. For example, he taught people to plant millet, beans, wheat and rice. So far, grain crops such as millet, sorghum and rice have been found in the remains of Yangshao Culture. The Yellow Emperor

气，还防鼠，便于随时取用，即便现在，用陶瓮贮存粮食也备受家庭主妇们的青睐。还有一种方法是修建大型的窖穴，把白膏泥涂抹在窖壁上或者烧烤坑壁都可以防潮。

农业发展了，家家都养得起牲畜，圈养牲畜可积聚大量肥料，施肥可以提高农作物产量，这样，种植业和饲养业相互促进，就成为仰韶文化时期农业发展迅速的原因之一。几乎在每个仰韶文化遗址，都可以看到零碎的家畜骨骼，有黄牛骨、鸡骨、猪骨。在各遗址中，猪骨都是最多的。猪是温顺、繁殖力旺盛的动物，生长快且易饲养，肉质鲜香肥美，还可为农业提供肥料。我们的祖先兴许那时就意识到了这一点，所以钟爱养猪。在裴李岗文化遗址中就出土了中国最早的艺术作品——陶塑猪，而中国最早的字典《说文解字》中对"家"字的解释就是房子下面有一头猪，是不是那时家家都养猪呢？对古人来说，圈养的猪能提供食物安全感，因此圈养生猪便成了定居生活的标志。

仰韶文化时期，河南地区的氏族社会是融合了炎帝和黄帝两族，尤其是以黄帝族为主的氏族社会。《史记》上说，炎帝传了八代之后才有了轩辕黄帝，可见，炎帝和黄帝都不是具体人名，而是两个不同部落首领的称号。黄帝在河南新郑定都，建立了有熊国。在今天的新郑，到处流传着有关黄帝的传说并存有与黄帝有关的遗迹。黄帝族在中原地区活动达2500余年，足迹遍及河南。黄帝曾在河南灵宝的荆山采矿冶铜，人们在仰韶文化晚期的遗址中发掘出了冶炼铜片，这是一项促使社会生产力飞速发展的重大技术发明，推动中国进入铜石并用的时代。中国许多著名的史书，如《史记》《汉书》《说文解字》等，都记载了黄帝在河南的功绩，与农业有关的是黄帝教人种黍、稷、菽、麦、稻。迄今，在河南的仰韶文化遗存中发现了粟、高粱和水稻等粮食作物。黄帝令部属制定天文历法。天文历法为农业生产和生活所必需，虽然现在不可能发现当时成文的历法，但在仰韶文化的大河村遗存中，发现了众多彩绘星象图，其中最引人注目的天象纹饰，如日纹、月纹、星纹、云纹、日

let his men make astronomical calendar, which is necessary for agricultural production and daily life. Although it is impossible to find the calendars of that time, many colored astrological pictures have been found on potteries in the remains of Dahe village in the period of Yangshao Culture. The most eye-catching celestial ornamentation, such as sun, moon, star, cloud, halo, solar prominence, constellation, etc., is the earliest astronomical material data found in China, reflecting Yangshao people's sensitive and meticulous observation of celestial phenomena. Solar halo and prominence are uncommon phenomena that signal some changes in weather, indicating that people already had some knowledge of astronomy and the calendar system. Zhouche — a means of transport — invented by the Yellow Emperor is no longer seen today. However, there were a lot of cultural similarities on the shores of the Yellow River during the period of Yangshao Culture, which indicates that the mutual exchanges were not blocked by the river. There was no doubt that Zhouche was credible to accelerate regional exchanges of agricultural knowledge and production implements. By the time of late Yangshao Culture, the clan society had undergone profound social changes, and the development of agriculture had been accelerating.

III. Ample Granaries in Ancient Times

Longshan Culture came into existence about 5,000 to 4,000 years ago. It was not firstly found in Henan Province, but in Longshan Town, Shandong Province. That's why it is given the name. However, archaeologists also found similar remains of Longshan Culture in Henan, which covers almost everywhere in today's Henan Province. In addition, Longshan Culture in Henan is different from that in Shandong. For example, Longshan Culture in Shandong mainly featured black pottery while most of the remains in Henan were made of grey pottery. Therefore, the Longshan Culture discovered in Henan is specifically known as "Henan Longshan Culture". At this period of time, the state started to take control of the whole society, and the early state economy developed unprecedentedly fast.

Comparatively, agriculture in the time of Henan Longshan Culture was more developed than that of Yangshao Culture, especially in the improvement of

河南郑州大河村遗址出土的太阳纹陶片
Painted pot shards with the sun pattern unearthed from Dahe village site, Zhengzhou City, Henan Province

晕纹、日珥纹、星座纹等，是中国目前发现最早的天文学实物资料，反映出当时的人们对天象非常敏感，观察很细致。日晕、日珥不是常见的现象，这些现象的出现，预示着天气要发生某种变化，说明那时的人们已有一定的天文知识和历法意识。黄帝发明了舟车，今天虽已不可见，但是仰韶文化时期，河流两岸，甚至黄河两岸的河南、河北都有非常多的文化共性，说明区域间的相互往来未被河流阻隔，有舟车是可信的。舟车的发明无疑会加快地区间农业知识和生产工具的交流。到了仰韶文化晚期，氏族社会已经发生了深刻的社会变革，农业加速向前发展。

三、到处都是粮仓

仰韶文化之后是龙山文化，距今5 000年至4 000年左右。龙山文化最早不是在河南省境内发现的，而是在山东省龙山镇发现的，因此叫龙山文化。但是考古学家在河南也发现了同类遗存，而且河南的龙山文化几乎覆盖了今天的河南省全境，又由于河南境内的龙山文化有不同于

production tools. For example, double-toothed wood Lei was used to turn over the soil, which was much more efficient than a stone spade. Although it was said that the Yan Emperor "cut down trees to make Si, bent wood to make Lei" in the period of Peiligang culture, it was only in the Longshan Culture sites that traces of their use could be discovered. This evidenced that Lei and Si were very popular in the period of Longshan Culture. In addition, the stone knife appeared in half-moon shape. Arc blade stone sickle, stone knife, mussel knife and mussel sickle were also widely used. What's more, the discovery of copper smelting slag and bronze fragments in many cultural sites of Longshan Culture in Henan suggests that the production efficiency was even higher as the result of tools production.

Diversion irrigation is an important advance in farming technology. Wells of this period were found in Tangyin County and Luoyang City, Henan Province. The best one was found in Tangyin County, 11 m in depth and 3.8 m in diameter. The well found in Luoyang City was connected to a canal. Well irrigation is an important measure to ensure crops yields in times of drought.

Archaeologists believe that Longshan people love making cellars. Great importance was attached to agriculture in the period of Henan Longshan Culture when the early state was forming. Crop varieties were still millet, sorghum and rice in this period of time. Although it is thought that rice is rarely grown on the north of the Yellow River, archaeological evidence shows that rice remains were unearthed from Yangshao Culture sites and Longshan Culture sites in the middle and lower reaches of the Yellow River. The planting area was expanded because people knew how to irrigate, and how to strengthen field management. As a result, grain yields increased exponentially. There was food surplus besides daily necessities. Therefore, methods adopted to handle the surplus food were: to store for later use, or to make wine. As Yangshao people did, Longshan people stored grains in a pottery pot, big in the middle and small at ends, both moisture-proof and rat-proof. However, small pottery pots were not enough to store grain, and big ones were needed. However, it was not easy to make big pottery pots and a house did not have enough space for so many big pottery pots. Hence, barn cellars become the best choice to store grain. It is no exaggeration to say that "Longshan people love making cellars" because several large and deep cellars were found in almost every Longshan Culture site in Henan Province. Each had its walls coated

河南淮阳平粮台遗址出土的蚌刀
Mussel knives unearthed from Pingliangtai site, Huaiyang District, Zhoukou City, Henan Province

山东龙山文化的特点，比如，山东龙山文化以黑陶为主要特征，河南遗存以灰陶居多，所以在河南发现的龙山文化被单独称为"河南龙山文化"。这个时期，国家政权初露端倪，整个社会被纳入国家控制轨道，早期的国家经济呈现出前所未有的发展态势。

河南龙山文化时期的农业比仰韶文化时期发达，首先表现在生产工具的改进方面。那时的人们用双齿木耒翻土耕地。这种工具掘土和翻土的效率比石铲高多了。虽然在裴李岗文化时期，传说炎帝"砍下树木做耜，折弯木头做耒"，但是只有在龙山文化遗址中看到了较多的使用痕迹，这说明当时木耒已非常普及。这个时候的石刀出现了半月形，还有弧刃石镰，石刀、蚌刀、蚌镰已被广泛使用。更重要的是，在河南的许多龙山文化遗存中都发现了炼铜渣和青铜残片，表明当时可能已开始制造生产工具，那样，生产效率就更高了。

引水灌溉是农耕技术的一项重大进步。在河南省汤阴县、洛阳市都发现了这个时期的井。汤阴有一口井，11米深，口径3.8米，是我国同

with white paste or straw mud, approximately 10 cm to 20 cm thick. Like pottery pots, they were small in entrance, spacious inside. The mouth of the cellars was usually 2 to 3 meters in diameter, big ones nearly 6 meters in diameter, and the depth of the cellars was usually 4 meters. Each barn cellar had an average storage of 1,000 kg grain, a big one even 10,000 kg. This reflects the high grain output and large surpluses in the period of Henan Longshan Culture. However, this could be only the rich's life, since private ownership and social inequality existed.

When it comes to wine-making, Henan has a long history. The world's earliest materials related to wine were found in Jiahu site. As early as 8,000 years ago, Jiahu people began to make fermented beverages. In the period of Longshan Culture, Henan's surplus grain provided the material foundation for wine-making industry. Just looking at wine vessels, the various types tell how much Henan people are fond of wine. The production of wine vessels really reached a very high level at that time. In addition to the usual wine vessels, bowls, cans, pots, there were many other types.

Animal husbandry had enjoyed unprecedented prosperity in the period of Longshan Culture, mainly in the form of raising pigs, dogs, cattle, sheep and chickens. The main movable property was domesticated animals and grains. The number of domestic animals was a symbol of a farmer's property. Thereafter, the concept of "having a bumper grain harvest and thriving domestic animals" has been unchanged for three or four thousand years in the history of traditional Chinese agriculture.

The period of Longshan Culture coincides with the time when the Yellow Emperor's descendants Zhuanxu, Ku, Yao, Shun and Yu, who were traditionally regarded as the human primogenitors of the Chinese nation, worked, lived and multiplied on the fertile land in Henan Province. With little doubt, they were historical representatives of this period in the history of Chinese civilization because the time, the region and the deeds of these heroes' activities were basically consistent with the archaeological findings.

It is said that the social order was seriously out of balance when Zhuanxu came to power. Everyone worshiped different spirits, but not the God of Heaven and the God of Earth. People were even uncomfortable with farming. In order to solve these problems, Zhuanxu carried out religious reforms. As a result, social

期最好的井。洛阳发现的井旁还有一条水渠与井连接。天旱缺水时，引井水灌溉，这是保证农作物收成的重要措施。

"龙山人好打洞"是考古学家爱说的一句话。正在形成早期国家的河南龙山文化时期，对农业非常重视。农作物品种依然是粟、高粱、水稻。尤其是水稻，以前人们总有一种错觉，认为黄河以北很少种植水稻，但考古证明，黄河中下游从仰韶文化时期到龙山文化时期都有稻米遗存出土。种植面积扩大了，人们懂得灌溉，知道加强田间管理，粮食产量成倍增加。当粮食有较多剩余时，人们就采取两种处置方法：贮存和酿酒。像仰韶文化时期一样，他们把粮食贮藏到两头小中间大的陶瓮里，既防潮又防鼠。不同的是，粮食太多，小陶瓮不够用，就烧制大陶瓮，但是烧制大陶瓮技术难度大，而且家里也放不下那么多大陶瓮，于是，挖窖穴贮藏粮食成为最好的办法。粮食多了，处处都是存粮的窖穴，说"龙山人好打洞"一点儿也不夸张，因为每个河南龙山文化遗址中都能发现若干个又大又深的窖穴，里面用白泥膏或草拌泥涂抹，涂层有10厘米到20厘米厚。像陶瓮一样，它们入口小，里面大，像个布袋，一般口径2米至3米，大的口径接近6米，深达4米，每个窖穴平均贮粮一千公斤，大的上万公斤。这种现象反映出河南龙山文化时期粮食产量较高，余粮多。不过，也可能只集中在富人身上，因为那时已经出现私有制，社会贫富不均现象已经存在。

说到酿酒，河南的酿酒历史源远流长，贾湖遗址有世界上最早与酒有关的实物资料，早在8 000年前，贾湖先民就开始酿造饮用发酵的饮料。龙山文化时期，河南粮食富余，为酿酒业提供了物质基础，只看酒器种类便可知河南人对于酒的钟爱程度。那时酒器制作已经达到很高水平，酒杯的种类繁多，除一般的盛酒器杯、盂、碗、罐、瓮等，还有温酒用的鬶、盉、斝等。

龙山文化时期的饲养业空前兴旺，人们主要饲养猪、狗、牛、羊、鸡五畜。家畜与粮食构成主要动产，家畜的多少是农家拥有财产多少的

order was restored. He also urged people to follow the natural laws in farming and encouraged them to open up cropland. In order to run the country, Zhuanxu made a clear division of the Chinese region for the first time, and set up Jiu Zhou (nine prefectures), some of which are still in use today. Zhuanxu also invented a calendar, known as *Zhuanxu Calendar*, which divides the four seasons according to calculations and delineations of the heavenly bodies. Di Ku (Emperor Ku), the Yellow Emperor's great-grandson, established the capital in Shangqiu, Henan Province. During the reign of Di Ku, he advocated that farming should be the first in all walks of life. On the basis of *Zhuanxu Calendar*, he divided a year into solar terms to guide people's farming in accordance with the seasons, which enabled the Chinese farming civilization to enter a new era.

Presumably, Yao (Emperor Yao) succeeded to the throne in the late period of Henan Longshan Culture. He set up a lot of official posts, and the country became prosperous and people were rich. According to position changes of the sun, the moon and the stars, he also worked out a calendar with 366 days for a year, with the leap month to adjust change of the four seasons—spring, summer, autumn and winter. Thereafter, Shun expanded the territory, Yu controlled the water, and Houji, worshiped as God of Grains, initiated people into growing millet and wheat.

IV. Artifacts of Farming

Three unearthed artifacts are very impressive from the Peiligang cultural site and Yangshao cultural site: Jia hu Gu Di (Jiahu crane bone flutes) unearthed from Jiahu village, Wuyang County, Henan Province, Guan Yu Shi Fu Tu Cai Tao Gang (Jar showing a stork with a fish and a stone axe) unearthed from Yan village, Ruzhou City, Henan Province, Cai Tao Shuang Lian Hu (Painted pottery connected-pots) unearthed from Dahe village, Zhengzhou City, Henan Province. Although they were made at different times in three different places of Henan Province, they were all closely related to agricultural activities.

Jiahu crane bone flutes are currently the oldest musical instruments found in China. Dating back to about 8,000 years ago, Jiahu people were very skillful in making crane bone flutes. They were able to get cranes, to accurately open holes, to

象征，这种观念在后来整个传统农业的三四千年间一直保持不变，那就是"五谷丰登，六畜兴旺"！

龙山文化时期是传说中的黄帝族后裔颛顼、帝喾、尧、舜、禹生活的时期，这些中华人文始祖都曾在河南这块沃土上奋斗、繁衍。由于这些英雄人物的活动时间、地域、事迹与考古发现基本相符，他们作为整个历史时期的代表人物是可信的。

传说颛顼初在位时，社会秩序严重失衡，百姓家家祭祀，人人祭神，不再敬地祭天，也不专心从事农业生产。为解决这个问题，他改革宗教，使社会恢复正常秩序，又劝导百姓从事农业生产要遵循自然规律，鼓励人们开垦田地。为治理天下，颛顼帝首次对中国区域进行明确划分，设立九州，部分设置沿用至今。颛顼帝还制定了历法，后人称其为《颛顼历》，按照太阳的周天行度，划分四季。帝喾是黄帝的曾孙，在河南商丘定都，他在位时，倡导百业以农为首，并在《颛顼历》的基础上定节气，划分了四时节令，指导人们按照节令从事农业生产，使华夏农耕文明走进一个崭新的时代。

大约在河南龙山文化后期，尧继位，他设了很多官职，国富民丰。他根据日月的出没、星辰的位次制定历法，一年有366天，用闰月的办法来校正春夏秋冬四季。此后帝舜扩土开疆，帝禹疏导治水，后稷被奉为谷神，教民耕种。

四、与农业活动息息相关

在裴李岗文化遗址和仰韶文化遗址上出土了三件令人难以忘怀的器物，一件是河南舞阳县贾湖遗址出土的骨笛，一件是河南汝州市阎村出土的鹳鱼石斧图彩陶缸，还有一件是河南郑州大河村出土的双连壶。它们诞生在河南不同时期的三个不同的地方，却都与农业活动息息相关。

贾湖骨笛是中国目前出土的年代最早的乐器实物。贾湖人在8 000

grind, and to calculate, etc. What's more, they also had a very good understanding of sounds and phonetic sequence. Jiahu people had found their way to satisfy their spiritual needs in the process of fighting against the nature. In the excavation of Jiahu site, the graves where crane bone flutes were found were larger than others and had more funerary objects, which led to speculation that the crane bone flutes were tools for wizards or the like to communicate with the heaven when there were some natural or human disasters during agricultural production or when they prayed for a good harvest. Since big cranes can fly to the sky, they were regarded as messengers to communicate between Heaven and Earth. However, cranes were not able to act on people's ideas. Thereupon, the ancients carved flutes from the wing bones of cranes, and made them sound like cranes to communicate with Heaven. Moreover, in the harvest year, crane bone flutes were used to accompany the song and dance. The sound of crane bone flutes was melodious and sweet, loud and clear, up to the sky, reporting people's gratitude to Heaven — the great god. More than 30 crane bone flutes were unearthed from Jiahu site, with 2, 5, 6, 7, and 8 flute holes respectively and different musical scales. Consequently, experts infer that they belonged to different stages in the history of music. As a matter of fact, crane bone flutes reflect a cultural phenomenon arising from the development of Jiahu agriculture, expressing the inhabitants' wishes and expectations.

Jar showing a stork with a fish and a stone axe was unearthed in 1978 from Yan village, Linru County (now Ruzhou City), Henan Province. It's said to be a funerary object, 47 cm high. It belongs to the Yangshao Culture in the Neolithic Age. The pictures of a stork, a fish and a stone axe are on the external wall, taking up half of the superficial area of the jar. The stork stands upright firmly on its six toes, with its raised head and wide-open eyes on the left, holding a large fish in its mouth, while to the right is a stone axe bound to a wooden handle. The painting is authentic and vivid, simple and elegant. This is the earliest and largest painted pottery ever found in China.

Stone axe, a common tool in the Neolithic Age, was used to cut down thistles and thorns, to make farmlands, and to defend against predators, which plays a great role in the struggle of primitive men to conquer and change nature. Thereupon, stone axe was naturally worshiped. The stone axe in the painting is elaborately designed. It does not lay flat casually, but stands firmly on the right

河南舞阳县贾湖遗址出土的骨笛
One of crane bone flutes unearthed from Jiahu site, Wuyang County, Henan Province

年前已经具备制造骨笛的全部本领：要得到鹤，要有精确开孔、磨平、计算等一系列工艺流程，并且还要有相当水平的对音、音序的理解能力。贾湖人在与大自然拼搏的过程中，已经开始寻找满足精神需求的途径。在舞阳贾湖遗址的发掘中，凡是出土骨笛的墓葬，墓穴都相对较大，随葬品也相对多一些。这不由得让人猜测，骨笛是从事巫术的人或者被称作"智人"的人用来与天沟通的工具，因为人们在农业生产中遇到天灾人祸或祈求好收成时都需要和天对话。鹤是能飞到天上的大鸟，是可以沟通天与凡界的使者，但是鹤不能依照人的意念行事，于是，古人就用鹤的尺骨制作成骨笛，令其发出鹤鸣来与天沟通。而在丰收的年景，骨笛更是被用来伴歌伴舞，骨笛声声，悠扬婉转，直冲云霄，向天汇报臣民对伟大的神的感恩。在已发掘的贾湖遗址中共出土骨笛三十多支，笛孔有2、5、6、7、8之别，具备不同的音阶，专家以此推断它们属于音乐史上不同的发展阶段。骨笛是贾湖农业发展过程中产生的文化现象，它最先反映的就是农民的意愿和农民的期盼。

鹳鱼石斧图彩陶缸出土于河南省汝州市阎村新石器时代仰韶文化遗址。据说这个陶缸是一件葬器，高47厘米，陶缸外壁一侧绘制有鹳鱼石斧图，这幅图占去缸体表面一半的面积。左绘有鹳鸟一只，昂首挺立，

with blade outward, showing its seriousness and mighty power. Since the stone axe was apparently endowed with power, it became a totem for the clan to accept people's worship. Stork in the painting is a beneficial bird that would bring the primitive clan with happiness and luck. The stork holding a fish toward the axe means that people offer sacrifices to the axe and that people pray for peace, auspiciousness, happiness and harvest of the clan.

Yangshao Culture is featured by typical painted pottery. Yangshao artisans created fine pottery with animal, plant and geometric designs in black and red pigment, which wouldn't peel off after baking. Painted pottery connected-pots unearthed from Dahe village, Zhengzhou City have been honored as the best of ancient painted pottery in China. Two pots are put side by side and connected by a circular hole. The pots have round body and flat bottom. They are made of red clay, painted in black parallel lines all over the body. According to some experts, painted pottery connected-pots are a wine set used at significant ceremonial events or national alliance, shared by the tribal leaders or elders to express their mutual hope for peace, friendliness, respect and love.

河南郑州大河村遗址出土的双连壶
Painted pottery connected-pots unearthed from Dahe village site, Zhengzhou City, Henan Province

河南汝州市阎村出土的鹳鱼石斧图彩陶缸
Jar showing a stork with a fish and a stone axe unearthed from Yan village, Ruzhou City, Henan Province

六趾抓地，二目圆睁，口含一条大鱼；右绘一把石斧，斧头捆绑在竖立的木棒上端。画面真实生动，色彩和谐，古朴优美，极富意境，是迄今中国发现最早、面积最大的一幅陶画。

石斧是新石器时代人们普遍使用的生产工具。人们用石斧砍倒荆棘，开辟田地，用石斧防御猛兽袭击，保护自身安全。石斧在原始人征服、改造大自然的斗争中发挥了巨大作用。自然，原始人对石斧产生了崇拜心理。画面上的石斧是经过作者精心加工处理的，它并不是被随意平放，而是巍然屹立在画面右边，斧刃朝外，形象严肃，一丝不苟，显示出巨大的威力，石斧显然被赋予了灵性，象征着权力。它已成为氏族图腾，接受人们的顶礼膜拜。画面上的鹳是能给原始氏族带来欢乐、吉祥的益鸟。鹳衔着大鱼，虔诚地面对石斧，代表着人向石斧奉献供品，祈求石斧保佑氏族平安、吉祥、欢乐、丰收。

仰韶文化时期是典型的彩陶文化时期，在器胎上用黑色和红色颜料描绘动植物或几何图纹，烧后不会脱落。在绚丽斑斓的彩陶器中，郑州

With the development of farming, fishing and hunting in primitive society, conflicts and wars often occurred between tribes and clans, which resulted in inhabitants' sufferings and great damage to their living environment as well. This forced the tribal leaders to reflect and realize that equality, communication, unity and alliance ought to be their common wishes and ideals. Therefore, they shared a pot of wine to pursue peace. Painted pottery connected-pots are connected by two pots with the same height, symbolizing the equal status of tribes and clans. Two pots are coupled together by a circular hole, symbolizing the communication between tribes and clans, sharing development and prosperity. Two pots are joined up with each other, symbolizing the tribes and clans would live in harmony and build a beautiful homeland together. The black paintings on two pots are different. One has parallel lines with vertical short lines. Another has parallel lines with oblique short lines. Experts speculated that the different patterns were supposed to stand for different tribes, and made it easy to identify when two people were drinking together at the same time. The connected-pots were regarded as a symbol and treasure of peace by our ancestors. This drinking custom with the connected-pots is still kept in some ethnic minorities up to now.

V. *Xia Xiao Zheng* : the Earliest Extant Chinese Calendar

Xia Xiao Zheng is said to be the calendar of the Xia Dynasty.

Xia clan, a branch of the descendants of the Yellow Emperor, sprung up around the period of the Longshan Culture in Henan Province. Xia clan settled in the areas of Songshan Mountain and the Luohe River, near the Youxiong Kingdom in the reign of the Yellow Emperor. After Yu the Great harnessed the water, the vast land was free of flood, so people could move out of the barren hills and highlands to the fertile plains. Here the plantation of crops and the raising of livestock promoted the agricultural development in central China. Yu the Great, for his great deeds of harnessing water, was respected and supported by Xia clan and its nearby clans or regional states, and was enthroned by Shun the Great at his old age. After conquering the nearby clans and states, Yu the Great built the Xia Dynasty in Henan Province.

In the Xia Dynasty, the nation paid great attention to water conservancy and

大河村仰韶文化遗址出土的彩陶双连壶被誉为中国古代彩陶之冠。双连壶两壶并列，相连处有一圆孔相通，圆腹平底，泥质红陶，器表满布平行线条。据专家考证，彩陶双连壶为神圣礼仪用品，是民族结盟或重大礼仪活动时部落首领、长者共饮的酒具，以表达和平、友好、相敬、相亲的意思。

随着原始社会农耕、渔猎的发展，部落之间、氏族之间矛盾冲突、战乱时常发生，给不同部落先民的生存环境造成巨大损害，战乱带来的身心苦痛迫使部落首领反省，平等、沟通、联合、结盟成了人们共同的心愿和理想。于是，人们常以酒化干戈，以酒为盟。彩陶双连壶，两壶一体，一体两壶，两壶一样高，象征着部落之间、氏族之间的平等；两壶相通，象征着沟通、交流，彼此共生共荣；两壶相连，象征着和谐相处，共建美好家园。双连壶左右两壶的黑彩图案各不相同，一个是平行线夹竖短线，另一个是平行线夹斜短线。专家推测不同的图案应该是代表着不同的部落，使用时两人共执此壶，同时饮用，不同的图案便于辨认。双连壶是祖先祈求和平的信物和宝物。这种双壶饮酒习俗在现在的少数民族中仍有沿用。

五、《夏小正》——中国现存最早的农事历书

《夏小正》相传为夏代遗留之物候及农事历书。

夏部族是黄帝族后裔的一支，约兴起于河南龙山文化时期，定居在离黄帝的有熊国不远的嵩山和洛水一带。禹治水成功后，广大地区免除水患，百姓能够从贫瘠的丘陵高地搬迁到肥沃的平原上安居乐业，植谷蓄畜，中原等地区的农业生产得到很大发展。禹治水有功，受到夏部族及周边部族或方国的尊重与拥戴，这样，舜在年迈的时候就选择了禹做王位继承人。禹征服了周边众多小国，在河南揭开了夏王朝历史的第一幕。

agricultural development, and therefore, the social economy grew fast. The relation between agriculture and phenological season became closer. Although a common calendar was employed in the Xia Dynasty, the application of the calendar in different regional states and clans was quite different—various sowing dates in different places, measuring the dates by trees or by stars or watching the growth of animals and plants—which resulted in different agricultural seasons. There was a great need for formulating a prevailing calendar in the whole nation. *Xia Xiao Zheng*, the earliest Chinese calendar, was written and handed down until today. *Xia Xiao Zheng* was written in the Warrior States Period rather than in the Xia Dynasty. Because the calendar was formulated in the Xia Dynasty, it was entitled *Xia Xiao Zheng*.

Xia Xiao Zheng, noted with the succession of twelve months, recorded the changes of phenological season, concerning celestial phenomena, meteorology, the changes of animals and plants as well as farming activities. In *Xia Xiao Zheng*, celestial phenomena recorded the changes of dask, dawn and horoscope in each month; meteorology recorded winds, rainfalls and temperatures in each season; plants covered the common herbs and woody plants; animals were about insects, fish, birds and mammals; farming activities referred to all kinds of agricultural production activities such as the planting of crops, fiber plants and horticultural crops and agricultural management thoughts. In addition, the activities of animal husbandry, sericulture, collection, fishing and hunting were first recorded. Here is the quotation about Zhengyue (the first month of the lunar year) from *Xia Xiao Zheng*:

In Zhengyue, hibernating worms awoke; wild geese flied north; pheasants sang; temperature rose; fish swam from underwater to the surface; glare ice flew in the river; the Chinese chive sprouted in the garden; rats came out of their holes; otters began catching fish; there were too many fish for otters to eat and some were left on the bank, just like sacrifice; hawks went away while turtledoves came; willows grew catkins; plums, apricots, mountain peaches bloomed; chimera grasses ripened; hens lain eggs.(This is about phenology.)

Ju star (Bowing star) appeared in the sky; three stars in the center of Shen Xiu sparkled in south; the handle of the Big Dipper points downward. (This is about celestial phenomena.)

进入夏王朝，社会经济快速发展，国家重视兴修水利，发展农业。农业与物候时令的关系愈加密切。当时虽然有了通行的历法，然而在应用上，各方国、各大族却自行其是，比如播种日期，有的靠树木测天，有的靠观察星象，有的通过观察动植物的生长等，农业时令很难达成一致，制定一部全国通用的历法成为时代的要求，于是产生了流传至今的《夏小正》——中国现存最早的农事历书。《夏小正》并非夏人所做，成书于战国时期，因保存的是夏代的历法，为尊重夏人而名之。

"夏小正"意思是夏代的农事，该书以全年十二个月为序，逐月记载物候变化，其内容涉及天象、气象、植物和动物变化、农事活动等方面。天象的内容为每个月的昏旦星象变化；气象包括各个时节的风、降雨、气温等；植物的内容涉及常见的草本和木本植物；动物的内容涉及昆虫、鱼类、鸟类和哺乳类动物；农事活动包括各个季节从事的各种农业生产活动，如谷物、纤维植物、园艺作物的种植以及农业管理思想。畜牧、蚕桑、采集、渔猎等均首次见于记载。这里先引述"正月"这部分，以见大概：

正月：启蛰。雁北乡。雉震响。鱼陟负冰。农纬厥耒。囿有见韭。时有俊风。寒日涤冻涂。田鼠出。农率均田。獭祭鱼。鹰则为鸠。采芸。鞠则见。初昏参中。斗柄悬在下。柳稊。梅杏杝桃则华。缇缟。鸡桴粥。

《夏小正》文字极简奥、古老，大多是二字或三字一句，再加上时间的推移，今人读起来觉得有些难度。可以想象，早在3 000多年前，古人就能用如此简练的文字归纳总结和记录全年的星象和物候现象，这是何等不容易。该书记载的星象位置经有关专家研究，证明是从夏代到商代都可以观察到的现象，这在后来的许多典籍中都得以印证，其所记载的内容和所观察的范围是后来二十四节气形成的基础，是古人在气象物候方面取得的里程碑式的成就。《夏小正》一书为我们研究中国古代天文及农耕文明的进步历程提供了极其宝贵的文字资料。

It was time to repair farm tools, such as lei Si (ancient spade-shaped tools used for tilling). It was time for the farmers to farm lands. (This is about farming activities.)

Xia Xiao Zheng, extremely concise in wording, profound in meaning, is very difficult for us to read today for its two-or-three-Chinese-character sentence structure. What a wonder! It is quite tough for people of three thousand years ago to record star and phenological phenomena of the year by concise wording. The places of stars recorded in *Xia Xiao Zheng* were observed by people in the Xia and Shang dynasties, which is confirmed by experts today. The later coming classics also gave an account of such places of stars. Its recording forms a sound base for the 24 solar terms. This is a landmark achievement made by ancient Chinese about stars and phenological phenomena. It has made great contributions to the study on the development process of ancient Chinese astronomy and farming civilization.

第二章

孜孜以求——河南传统农业

Chapter II

Traditional Agriculture

传统农业是相对于原始农业和现代农业而言的完全以农民世代使用的各种生产要素为基础的农业，是人类文明史上持续时间最长、涉及范围最广、社会影响最深的经济形式或经济社会现象。传统农业相对于原始农业的进步在于：其一，劳动工具的改善，促进了生产力的发展。铁器的广泛使用，铁犁与畜力的结合，改变了刀耕火种的生产方式，大大提高了劳动生产率，并为扩大耕作面积、大幅度增加农产品产量创造了条件。其二，生产经验的积累，提高了人类利用自然的能力，创造了人工施肥、提高肥力的增产措施。其三，创造了选择农作物和牲畜良种的办法，改善了农作物和牲畜生产的状况。其四，创立了间作套种等复种耕作制度。尽管传统农业的技术进步十分缓慢，但经过长期积累而形成的农业技术，能较好地适应当地的自然和社会经济条件，有些技术一直沿用至今。龙山文化（距今5 000—4 000年）的中晚期，相当于远古传说中的黄帝至尧舜禹时代，以黄河流域为中心的中原地区的原始农业就开始逐步向古代的传统农业过渡。传统农业经历了从史前文明时代到18世纪中叶大约数千年的发展历程，中国的传统农业技术一直走在世界前列，在这个漫长的过程中，河南是中国传统农业的主力军。

一、青铜农具的发轫

商的始祖契曾经协助大禹治水，创下功绩，被舜封于商，在今天河南北部。他们善耕、善牧，更善于经商。契的孙子相土驯马拉车，驮货到很远的地方进行交易，促进了商族经济的发展。契的后代汤在商族首领中最为杰出，他任人唯贤，赏罚分明，势力日大，诸侯纷纷归附，渐渐成为夏朝东方一个强大的方国。其时，夏朝暴君桀当政，荒淫奢靡，鱼肉百姓，人民怨声载道。汤就此用兵征伐，一举灭掉延续了约400年的夏朝，建立了商王朝。商王朝势力浩浩荡荡，就像《诗经》上记载的一样："昔有成汤，自彼氐羌。莫敢不来享，莫敢不来王。"商汤定都

Compared with the primitive and modern agriculture, the traditional agriculture is entirely based on the various factors of production used by farmers from generation to generation. It is a form of economy and social phenomenon which is of far-reaching significance in the history of human civilization. The traditional agriculture made great progress: firstly improvement of labor tools promoted the agricultural productivity. The widespread use of iron farm tools and the combination of iron ploughs and animal forces shifted the slash-and-burn production method, promoted agricultural productivity, and provided a solid foundation for enlarging farming areas and greatly increasing produce. Secondly, the accumulation of farming experiences improved the capacities in utilizing natural resources, such as artificially applying fertilizers to improve soil fertility. Thirdly, the new method of cultivating crops and livestock improved the traits of crop and livestock production. Fourthly, the traditional agriculture adopted the system of intercropping, interplanting and multiple cropping. Although the traditional agriculture techs improved quite slowly, the framing techniques which are formed through the long-term accumulation of farming experiences, adapted to the local and social as well as economic resources, some of which were handed down till today. The late period of Longshan Culture (about 5000 BC-4000 BC) witnessed the transition of the the primitive agriculture of the central China, with the Yellow River basin as the center, to the traditional agriculture. The traditional agriculture lasted from then on to the middle of 18th century. The Chinese traditional agriculture techniques took the lead in the world. Henan was the main force of the Chinese traditional agriculture.

Ⅰ. The Origin of Bronze Farming Tools

Xie, the ancestor of Shang people, helped Yu the great harness water. Xie was given Shang (the north of Henan Province today) as a reward for his service by Shun Emperor, and therefore Xie's descendants were called Shang people, who were good at farming, hunting and doing business. Xiangtu, Xie's grandson, tamed horses to pull goods to trade with faraway people. Business trading promoted economic development. Tang, the generation of Xie, was the greatest leader among Shang people. He appointed people according to their ability and political integrity and ruled his men with ample reward and punishment, so his kingdom became quite strong and other prefectures were attached to Shang one

西亳（河南偃师），后迁都至郑州。此后，商又多次迁都，直至商王盘庚迁都到殷，也就是今天的河南安阳。

在郑州商城和安阳殷墟都发现有大型青铜制造作坊，从发掘的陶范数量看，铸造青铜生产工具的陶范多于青铜容器的陶范，由此可见商代前期对农业生产的重视。不过在河南境内发现的青铜农具数量并不多，有铜钁、铜铲，主要发现的农具还是木器、石器、骨器和蚌器。这并不奇怪，铜器毕竟贵重，而且可传世和重新回炉再铸。另外，一般平民也买不起，即使拥有，也舍不得丢弃，因为坏了会再次熔铸，也舍不得随葬墓中。还有一个原因是河南地区处在黄河中下游，绝大部分在黄土覆盖范围内，土质松软，木器使用起来轻巧方便，造价也不高。不管怎么说，这个时期的农业发展有多方面的因素，农具只是农业生产效能的一种标志，不能仅仅从考古出土的工具数量来判断当时的农业生产情况。在商代乃至后来的西周时代，青铜农具的数量和质量都没有达到左右农业发展的程度，重要的是，青铜用于农具制造，改变了石、木、蚌、骨垄断农具制造五六千年的局面，迎来了金属用于农具制造的新时代，其社会意义是深远的。

二、甲骨上的商代农业

安阳殷墟出土的甲骨文震惊世界。甲骨文是镌刻或写在龟甲和兽骨上的文字，出土于河南安阳小屯一带，这里曾是商代后期的都城，史称"殷"。商朝人大都迷信鬼神，大事小事都要卜问，有些占卜的内容是关于天气的，有些是农作收成，也有问病痛、求子的，而打猎、作战、祭祀等大事更是需要问卜了。

甲骨文所记述的内容不仅让商史成为信史，而且甲骨文所反映的商代社会经济生活的方方面面，使得我们对那时候的农业也有了新认识。据统计，经过整理的殷墟出土的甲骨卜辞，与农业生产或农业礼俗有

after another. At that time, Jie, emperor of the Xia Dynasty was cruel and his people wanted to abandon him. Tang destroyed the Xia Dynasty by attacking on it. The *Shi Jing* (*The Book of Songs*) goes like "There used to be Tang, of Di&Qiang people. All the people at that time had an audience with Tang, the emperor". Tang selected Xibo (Yangshi County, Henan Province now) as the capital of Shang Dynasty and then moved the capital to Zhengzhou. Thereafter, Shang's capitals were moved from places to places till Yin (Anyang City in Henan Province now) by Pangeng (an emperor in Shang Dynasty).

Many large bronze workshops were found in Zhengzhou City and Yin Ruins of Anyang City. From the perspective of unearthed pottery molds, there were more bronze tools besides bronze vessels, which means the early Shang Dynasty paid more attention to farming. The number of unearthed bronze tools in Henan Province was not large, such as Jue and bronze spades. The main unearthed farming tools were made of other materials, wood, stone, bone and mussels. The very high price of bronze might account for this phenomenon. In general, common people couldn't afford the bronze tools or containers. Even if bronze tools or containers were broken, they would not like to discard and were reluctant to bury the bronze tools or containers with the dead. Another reason may be that most part areas of Henan Province is located in the middle and lower reaches of the Yellow River, most areas of which are loess covers, soft and easy for cheap wooden tools. What really matters is that the bronze tools shifted the monopolization of stone tools, wooden tools, mussel tools and bone tools, which even had existed for five thousand to six thousand years. The new era of bronze tools had a significant social influence.

II. Agriculture of Shang Dynasty Recorded in Oracle Bones

The world is shocked by the unearthed oracle bone inscriptions in Yin Ruins of Anyang City. Oracle bone inscriptions are old Chinese characters written or carved on tortoise shells and animal bones, unearthed in Xiaotun village, Anyang City, Henan Province. Anyang City was the capital of Shang Dynasty from Emperors of Pangeng to Dixin, called Yin in history. Most people in the Shang Dynasty were superstitious about ghosts and gods. They practised divination almost on every aspect, such as weather, produce, pains and ills, birth, hunting, war as well as sacrifice.

The contents of oracle bone inscriptions make the history of Shang Dynasty

关的有四五千片之多,可以大致分为农作物类、农田治理类、作物种植类、田间管理类、收割与储藏类、占卜粮食收成丰歉类以及巫师占卜求雨类等。

《甲骨文合集》编号09994:……［受］黍年。"黍"是谷物的一种,现在北方人称其为糜子或"大黄米"。古人把谷物的收成视为神灵授予的。上面说的"［受］黍年",就是向神灵问卜,种"黍"能不能得到好收成。在卜辞中有很多这样的问卜,"受稷年""受麦年""受菽年"等,都是就具体的农作物向神灵占卜求得好收成,我们因此可以推知商代的农作物都有些什么。甲骨卜辞中出现了黍(糜)、稷(粟、谷)、麦、菽(大豆)、秜(稻)、畲(高粱)。甲骨文中这几个字几乎都有多种写法,有的指同类作物,有的则指同类作物不同品种,如"麦",有"来"和"麦",古文字学家说前者指"大麦或青稞",后者指"小麦",可见当时粮食作物品种已经很多了。单说小麦,小麦起源于西亚及地中海东岸地区。甲骨卜辞上告诉我们至少在殷商时代,或是更早的某个时候,小麦已传入中国,且主要在黄河中下游的中原地区种植。小麦在先秦时期还不是主食,而是昂贵稀有之物,只有贵族、宫廷才食用。甲骨卜辞中数次出现的"告麦"二字,是侯伯之国要把丰收的喜讯告知殷王之意。先秦时,人们尚不知将小麦磨成面粉,也就不容易下咽。直到西汉,政府才提倡种植,并且一跃成为仅次于水稻的第二大类粮食作物。

殷商时,统治者高度重视农业。卜辞中有商王亲自视察农业生产的记录。编号137:己亥卜,贞王观籍。释义:问商王是否可亲往观看耕作。编号138:庚子卜,贞王其观籍更往。十二月。释义:问商王要亲自观看耕籍吗?编号139:弜籍乘萑(获)其受有年。释义:麦类收获后暂不翻耕会影响收获否?此外,巫师也可作法,如甲骨文中有"其乍龙于凡田,有雨",意思是装扮成龙神,在凡地的田间跳化妆巫舞以求雨。

believable, but also reflect every aspect of Shang Dynasty in social lives and economy, and thus we can have a clear idea of agriculture in Shang Dynasty. According to the statistics, there are more than four thousand to five thousand pieces of oracle bones related to agriculture. The contents of these oracle bones usually go into the following: crops, farmland management, crop planting, harvesting and storage, divination on harvest and rains.

The Collection of Oracle Bones, No. 09994: Shou Shu Nian (divination on harvest of grains this year). Shu, one of grains, now called broom-corn millet or "Big Yellow Rice" (proso millet) in the north of China. The ancient Chinese regarded the harvest of grains as the endowment by the gods. There are many inscriptions like this one, such as "Shou Ji Nian (divination on the harvest of Ji, millet)", "Shou Mai Nian (divination on the harvest of wheat)" as well as "Shou Shu Nian (divination on the harvest of Shu, beans)". From these inscriptions, we can infer what crops were planted in Shang Dynasty. Shu (grain), Ji (millet), Mai (wheat), Shu (bean), Ni (rice), She (sorghum) appeared in the inscriptions. These characters have different spellings. Some refer to the similar crops while others refer to different varieties of similar crops. Mai (wheat) has two different spellings—"来" and "麦"; the former refers to barley or highland barley; the later refers to wheat. Wheat is an import of ancient times, originating in Western Asia and the eastern coast of the Mediterranean. Inscriptions say that wheat was imported to China in the Shang Dynasty or even earlier. Wheat was mainly planted in central China, that is the middle and lower reaches of the Yellow River. Wheat was not staple food in the pre-Qin Period. Only the noble or royal families could afford this rare and expensive wheat. The two characters "Gao Mai" appeared twice in inscriptions, which means king of kingdoms or lords of prefectures told the good news of wheat harvest to emperors of Shang Dynasty. In the pre-Qin Period, wheat was not yet ground to flour and hard to swallow. Until the Western Han Dynasty, the government began to advocate planting wheat, and wheat became the staple food, second only to rice.

In the Shang Dynasty, the rulers attached great importance to agriculture. No. 137 inscription shows the emperor personally inspected the conditions of agricultural production. The inscription says "Whether it is good for the emperor personally inspecting the conditions of agricultural production". No. 138 inscription goes "In December, do your Majesty the emperor inspect the conditions personally?" No. 139 inscription tells "Does it affect the next season's

大量与农业有关的卜辞说明农业在当时的社会经济中占据了非常重要的地位。除草杀虫是农业的重要内容，卜辞中就有关于商代农业虫害的记载，以及有求雨和驱虫害的卜辞。园艺方面，卜辞中已有表示"圃"的字。此外，卜辞中祭祀的名目繁多，祭祀用的牛羊数量非常多，这得益于商代畜牧业的发达。在卜辞中还有反映圈养动物的文字，说明在当时的畜牧业已不仅限于放牧。根据甲骨卜辞记载，以商王为首的统治集团几乎介入了谷类粮食作物种植的全部过程。在播种之前，要举行仪式；商王要及时发布农作命令，还要象征性地参加谷物播种及收割的过程，其实也是一种农事礼。总之，甲骨卜辞所反映的商代社会是典型的农业社会，国家以农为本，以农立国。商代所形成的农业礼俗与制度，对后世影响非常深远。

三、《诗经》与周代农业

殷商的农业情况大多反映在甲骨卜辞上，而西周的农业发展在《诗经》里反映得最为淋漓尽致。大家知道周朝分为很多个诸侯国，足有几百个之多。为了巩固王室统治，管理好天下，周天子就要了解民情，并且保证分封到各地的诸侯、贵族不为各地的方言、不同的习俗、不同的

《诗经》
Shi Jing

produce after harvesting the wheat without ploughing?" Another inscription also tells "The wizard can also implement the practice of rainfall".

Many inscriptions in oracle bone show that agriculture played an important role in social economy of the Shang Dynasty. Some inscriptions also record the activities of weeding, insect-killing as well as the practice of praying for rain. Gardening is even mentioned in the inscriptions. Characters about captive animals in the inscriptions indicate that animals were not limited to grazing. According to the oracle bone inscriptions, almost all the ruling groups headed by Shang emperors got themselves in the whole process of grain crop cultivation. Before planting, they would hold a ceremony; emperors of the Shang Dynasty should issue farming orders in time, and symbolically participate in the process of grain sowing and harvesting. In fact, it is also a kind of farming etiquette. In a word, the Shang Dynasty in the inscriptions of oracle bone was a representative of agriculture society. The whole nation took agriculture as its ruling foundation. Agricultural etiquette and systems formed in Shang Dynasty had far-reaching influence on later generations.

III. *Shi Jing* (*The Book of Songs*) and Agriculture in the Zhou Dynasty

The agricultural situation of the Shang Dynasty was mostly reflected in oracle bone inscriptions, and that of the Western Zhou Dynasty was most vividly reflected in *Shi Jing* (*The Book of Songs*). As is known to all, the Zhou Dynasty was divided into hundreds of prefectures. In order to consolidate the rule of the royal family and manage the whole nation of the Zhou Dynasty well, emperors had to hear his people's voices and ensure that the enfeoffed nobles were not alienated by the dialects, customs and cultures of different states. So in spring, emperors sent poetry collectors to collect poems with wooden handles, standing by the roadside or visiting from door to door. With the collected poems, emperors roughly grasped people's voices. The collected poems were classified, compiled and composed, the folk songs of the local places were classified as *Feng* (literally means wind, one section in *Shi Jing*), the music used in the imperial court was classified as *Ya* (literally means elegance, one section in *Shi Jing*), and the music used for religious sacrifice was called *Song* (literally means Song, one section in *Shi Jing*). *Shi Jing* was the first collection of poems in China, which recorded

文化所异化。于是，周天子就派采诗官在每年的春天，手执木铎站在田间路旁或挨门挨户去采诗。采诗官把采来的诗拿给周王看，周王对各地民情就可以掌握得八九不离十了。周人把采集来的诗加以归类、编纂、谱曲，属于乡土的民歌归为"风"，属于朝廷上用的音乐归为"雅"，属于宗教祭祀用的音乐称作"颂"。孔子编订了《诗经》，共收录了305篇，这样，《诗经》就成为中国第一部诗歌总集，它记录了殷商末年到春秋中叶上下五六百年的事情。《诗经》的产生跟周人的礼乐文化有着密切关系，而周人的礼乐又萌生于周的农业。孔子说"诗无邪"，梁启超说"唯有《诗经》是真金美玉"，可见《诗经》记录的真实性。那么，《诗经》里的周代农业是什么样子呢？

以《周颂·臣工》为例。

嗟嗟臣工，敬尔在公。王厘尔成，来咨来茹。嗟嗟保介，维莫之春，亦又何求？如何新畲？於皇来牟，将受厥明。明昭上帝，迄用康年。命我众人：庤乃钱镈，奄观铚艾。

这首诗是以周王的口气写的，他说：

群臣百官听我说，应当谨慎做公务。君王赐予你成法，需要研究再调度。农官你们也听令，正是暮春的节令，有何要求说来听，新田旧田如何种。今年麦子长势好，秋天将有好收成。光明无比的天神，赐我丰收好年景。农夫们：收起锄铲等农具，我要去视察开镰收割了！

周王朝在立国之初就制定了土地分配、土地管理、耕作制度的具体法规，把品种改良、土壤改良、水利建设以及轮种等耕作技术都包括在内。周人鼓励开垦土地，又注重土壤改良，田地被分成三种：一种休耕，称"菑（zī）田"，一种休耕后的称"新田"，还有一种属于休耕后连续耕种两年的称"畲（yú）田"。西周时，耦耕、轮番休耕、播种前的除草、掘挖沟洫引水排水、病虫害防治等各种生产技术都已齐备。周朝重祭祀，祭礼繁多，不但在开耕之前要向神明祈祷，而且在收获之后也向神明致谢。

the events from the end of the Shang Dynasty to the middle of the Spring and Autumn Period for five or six hundred years, totaling 305 poems. Hereupon,the birth of *Shi Jing* was closely related to Zhou people's ritual and music culture,and Zhou people's rituals and music originated in Zhou agriculture. Confucius said that "All poems in *Shi Jing* come from true feelings".Liang Qichao said,"only *Shi Jing* is the true gold and jade." This shows the authenticity of the records in *Shi Jing*.What was agriculture like in *Shi Jing* in the Zhou Dynasty?

An example (a poem given by emperor of the Zhou Dynasty) is taken here.

All officials attention! You should be cautious in your official duties. The emperor gives you the law, which needs to be studied and re-scheduled. Agricultural officials, you should also obey orders. It is the time of late spring, what you need should let me know as well as how to plant new fields and old ones. The wheat is growing well this year and there will be a good harvest in the autumn. The brightest God please give me a good harvest. My people: Pick up your hoe, shovel and other farm tools, I will go to inspect the harvest!

At the beginning of the Zhou Dynasty, it formulated specific laws and regulations on land allocation, land management and farming system, including varieties improvement, soil improvement, water conservancy construction and rotation farming techniques. People in the Zhou Dynasty were encouraged to reclaim the field and to pay attention to soil improvement. Fields were divided into three types: one was fallow field, called "*Zitian*", and one was "*Xintian*" (new field) after fallowing, the third one was continuous planting field for two years after fallowing, called "*Yutian*". During the Western Zhou Dynasty, various producing techniques were applied in farming, such as coupling tillage, alternate fallow tillage, weeding before sowing, digging ditches, drainage, pest control and so on. The Zhou Dynasty paid great attention to sacrifice by offering many sacrifices. They not only prayed to the gods before ploughing, but also thanked gods after harvest.

In *Shi Jing*, many poems described the vigorous development of agriculture in the Zhou Dynasty. In spring, tens of thousands of farmers ploughed together in the vast fields stretching over thirty *li*; in summer, thousands of people weeded and hoed together; in autumn, thousands of carriages carried grain back home. Grain piled up like mountains and granaries were fully filled. They brewed fine wine with new grains for their ancestors to taste and showed their gratitude to gods for their good fortune. Not only crops increased in great quantity, livestock, fishing and hunting, sericulture and other sideline also developed fast at the same

《诗经》里有很多作品都描述了周朝农业蓬勃发展的情况：春天，几万农夫在方圆三十余里的广阔原野上一起春耕；夏天，几千人一起锄草耘苗；秋天，千辆万辆的马车载谷而归，谷物堆积如山，粮食装满粮仓，他们用新粮酿造美酒献给祖先品尝，感谢上苍普降福禄多吉祥。不仅粮食作物丰收，畜牧、渔猎、养蚕等副业同时发展。周初，丝物中已有各色丝线。

总之，借助《诗经》的解读，我们对西周时期的农业生产及农业政策可以有比较全面的了解。

四、铁器、牛耕、水利与农家

公元前8世纪时，铁农具在河南地区出现。公元前17世纪，青铜农具的出现改变了石、木、蚌、骨垄断农具制造五六千年的局面，迎来了金属可以用于农具制造的新时代，这毫无疑问具有深远的社会意义。但是，严格意义上讲，青铜农具的出现并不能完全排挤掉石器。大约一千年后，铁农具的使用，才使石器、木器、铜器、蚌器等农具真正走下了历史舞台。铁农具和牛耕的使用，是中国古代农业发展的新的里程碑，它出现在西周之后的春秋战国时期。

春秋战国时期，井田制消失，土地逐渐私有化，生产管理方式出现变化，铁农具和牛耕的出现使得河南地区的农业生产方式和生产技术都有了质的变化。河南当地生产的铁农具种类特别多，有犁铧、镢、铲、锄、耑、镰、刀等。有了铁农具，人们干起活来格外得心应手。凡是拓荒、深翻土地、挖河引水灌溉，处处离不开铁农具的身影。在战国时期，牛耕普遍使用，这是耕作技术的一次重要改革，不仅解放了人力，还使耕作效率大大提高。牛耕是中华农业文明里必不可少的元素之一，直到2 800多年后的今天，中国的一些边远农村依然离不开铁农具和牛耕。

time. In the early Zhou Dynasty, there were all kinds of silk threads in colours.

In short, *Shi Jing* gives a comprehensive understanding of agricultural production and agricultural policies in the Western Zhou Dynasty.

Ⅳ. Ironware, Cattle Farming, Water Conservancy and Agriculturist

In the 8th century BC, iron farming tools appeared in Henan Province. In the 17th century BC, the emergence of bronze farm tools has changed the situation where stone, wood, mussel and bone monopolized farm tools for five or six thousand years, and ushered in a new era where metal could be used in manufacturing farm tools. Iron farming tools undoubtedly had far-reaching social significance. Strictly speaking, the emergence of bronze farming tools could not completely exclude stone farming tools. Therefore, about one thousand years later, the wide use of iron farming tools ended the use of stone, wood, bronze, clam and other farming tools. The use of iron farming tools and cattle farming was a milestone in the development of agriculture in ancient China which appeared in the Spring and Autumn Period and the Warring States Period after the Western Zhou Dynasty.

In the Spring and Autumn Period and the Warring States Period, with the disappearance of the Jingtian System , the land was privatized gradually. The agricultural production management changed. The appearance of iron farming tools and cattle farming resulted in qualitative changes of the agricultural production mode and production technology in Henan Province. There appeared many kinds of iron farming tools, such as ploughs, brackets, shovels, hoes, bowls, sickles, knives and so on. With iron farming tools, people were particularly skilled in their farming. Whenever pioneering, deep turning over land, digging rivers and diverting water for irrigation, iron farming tools were indispensable. During the Warring States Period, cattle farming was widely used, which was an important farming technology reform. It not only liberated human resources, but also greatly improved the farming efficiency. Cattle farming was one of the indispensable elements of Chinese agricultural civilization. Until today, more than 2,800 years later, in some remote rural areas of China, iron farming tools and cattle farming are still in place.

Suitable iron farming tools, and cattle farming that emancipated manpower from phisical work opened up a broad agricultural development prospects.

河南省辉县和山西长治出土的战国时期的铁农具
Various iron farming tools (during the Warring States Period), unearthed in Huixian City, Henan Province, and Changzhi City, Shanxi Province

得心应手的铁农具和负重劳作、解放人力的耕牛开辟了广阔的农业发展前景。河南在华北平原南部，夏天动辄暴雨，形成洪涝灾害；春、秋两季又少雨水，出现旱灾。过去人们基本靠天吃饭，春秋战国时期就不一样了，好多小国都纷纷兴修水利。

期思陂是中国历史上最早的水利工程之一，孙叔敖是这个工程的总设计师。孙叔敖一生政绩很多，但他最善于治水。古时，河南固始县一带雨量充沛，但排水不畅，常常形成洪灾。孙叔敖利用大别山北坡的来水，在泉河、石槽河上游将众多的陂塘沟堰贯通，修建成渠系，形成"长藤结瓜式"的期思陂，用于灌溉那一带的田野，从而形成著名的期思陂。这个工程不仅使当时的人们广为受益，也造福了后代。到明清时期，期思陂仍然发挥着作用。

200年后，在河南又流传起"西门豹治邺"的故事。战国时期，魏国政治家西门豹初到河南安阳一带任县令，看到这里人烟稀少，田地荒芜萧条，一片冷清，问其缘由，原来这里的漳河年年发大水，这里的县吏和巫神勾结，强征赋税，并强迫把穷人家的漂亮女孩投入河中，做"河神"的妻子。因此老百姓为避税避难都逃离这里。西门豹听后立志改变现状，后来趁"河神娶妻"的机会，惩治了地方恶霸势力，随后颁

Located in the south of North China Plain, Henan Province often suffered heavy rains in summer, resulting in floods and water logging disasters or droughts because of little rain in spring and autumn. Before the Spring and Autumn Period, people mainly depended on the weather for food. In the Spring and Autumn Period and the Warring States Period, water conservancy projects were built in many small states.

Qisi Bei (Qisi Irrigation Project) was the earliest water conservancy project in the history of China. Sunshu Ao was the chief designer of this project. Sunshu Ao made many achievements in his life, but he was the best at water harnessing. In ancient times, Gushi County, Henan Province, had abundant rainfall, but poor drainage, which often resulted in floods. Sunshu Ao used the water coming from the northern slope of the Dabie Mountain to build a canal system to irrigate the fields in that area. This project not only benefited the people at that time, but also the future generations. By the Ming and Qing dynasties, Qisi Bei still worked.

200 years later, another story about "Ximen Bao Harnessing the Ye" was popular in Henan Province. During the Warring States Period, Ximen Bao, a statesman of the Wei State, came to Anyang to serve as county magistrate. He saw here sparsely populated, a barren field of desolation. He learned that the Zhanghe River flooded every year and the county officials here colluded with witches to impose high taxes, and force pretty girls from poor families into the river to be wives of the River God. The common people for this reason flew away. After hearing this, Ximen Bao decided to change the status. Later, he punished the local bullies, and then issued a decree prohibiting witchcraft. Those who had previously left returned to their homes. At the same time, he personally led the people to survey water sources and mobilized the people to dig 12 canals on both sides of the Zhanghe River, which not only curbed the floods in the Zhanghe River, but also secured a large area of land a good harvest in case of drought or flood.

Honggou was another big canal excavated by men. The Yellow River water was introduced into the vicinity of Zhengzhou through Honggou which irrigated a lot of land around.

In the history of China, the Spring and Autumn period and the Warring States Period were the most brilliant periods of ideology and culture. During this period, Confucianism, Taoism, Legalism and other schools of thought contended with each other in an unprecedented academic situation, which played an important role in the development of Chinese thought. One of them is

布律令，禁止巫风，原先出走的人家也纷纷回到了自己的家园。同时，他又亲自率人勘测水源，发动百姓在漳河两岸开挖了12条水渠，不仅根治了漳河水患，也使大片田地成为旱涝保收的良田。

鸿沟是另一条人工开凿的大渠。黄河水通过鸿沟被引入郑州附近，灌溉圃田一带的许多土地。

中国历史上，春秋战国时期是思想和文化最为辉煌灿烂、群星闪烁的时期。这一时期出现了儒家、道家、法家等诸子百家相互争鸣、盛况空前的学术局面，在中国思想发展史上占有重要的地位。农家也是其中之一。

农家是先秦时期反映农业生产和农民思想的学术流派，代表人物是许行，他堪称下层农民的代言人。他认为统治者要体恤百姓疾苦，不可巧取豪夺，提出"顺民心""忠爱民"是一切统治的基础。他依托远古神农氏之言来宣传他的主张，推行耕战政策，发展农业生产，研究农业生产问题，关注农业灾害问题。农家认为，农业教人懂得道德教化，所以"农本商末"应该成为中国传统社会的一项基本国策。因为农业生产必须依赖阳光、雨水等气象条件，还要有供作物生长的土地，当然也少不了人发挥体力和智慧，因此提出"天—地—人"是一个最稳定的结构。由于当时的平民绝大多数都从事农耕，所以"重农"就是"重民"，重农倾向最终发展为民本思想。《吕氏春秋》中的《上农》讲的就是农家学派的重农政策，农业是富国强兵之本，而《任地》等三篇讲的是农业科技问题，主要反映以河南为中心的黄河流域农业的现状。

五、二十四节气

远古时期，中国的先民为了搞好农业生产，很注意掌握农时，因为只有掌握农时，按农时从事农事活动，农业生产才能获得好收成，掌握农时就是掌握节气气候的变化规律，于是产生了中国人引以为豪并沿用

Agriculturists.

The representative of agriculturist, an academic school reflecting agricultural production and farmers' thoughts in the pre-Qin Period, was Xu Xing who was also called the spokesman of the lower peasants. He advocated that rulers should be sympathetic to the sufferings of the people and should not take the plunder by chance. He proposed that "obeying the people's hearts" and "loving the people loyal" were the basis of all rule. He propagated his ideas in Shennongshi's words to carry out the policy of farming and warfare, reward developing agricultural production, study on agricultural production issues, and pay attention to agricultural disasters. Agriculturists believed that agriculture taught people moral education, so "agriculture-based, business-supressed" should become a basic national policy of traditional Chinese society. As agricultural production has to rely on meteorological conditions such as sunshine and rain, and land for crops to grow, as well as human strength and wisdom, it is proposed that "heaven-earth-human" is the most stable structure. Since most of the civilians were engaged in farming at that time, "attaching great importance to agriculture" meant "attaching importance to the people", and the tendency to lay stress on agriculture eventually developed into people-oriented thinking. "*Shang Nong*" in *Lüshi Chunqiu* (*Lü's Spring and Autumn Annals*) is about the policy of emphasizing agriculture. Agriculture is the base of enriching the country and strengthening the army, while "*Rendi*" and other two articles cover agricultural science and technology, which mainly reflected the situation of agriculture in Yellow River Basin centering around Henan Province at Lü's time.

V. The Twenty-four Solar Terms

In ancient times, in order to have a good harvest, Chinese ancestors paid great attention to farming season. Because only when they grasped the farming season and engaged in farming activities accordingly could they get a good harvest. To grasp the farming season means to grasp the changing law of the solar season and climate, which produced the twenty-four solar terms that the Chinese people were proud of and are still in use today.

The wise ancient Chinese erected an upright, fixed-length pole on the ground, and built a ridge in the north direction of the pole. The change of the length of the pole shadow was an important basis for measuring solar terms. When the sun

至今的二十四节气。

聪明的古人将一根直立的、长度固定的杆子立在地上,在杆子的下边向北的方向,修成一条土埂子,杆影长度变化就是测量节气的重要依据。当太阳升到中天,也就是正南方向时,太阳光照射在直立的杆子上,杆子的投影正好落在北面的土埂子上。冬天和夏天太阳照射角度不一样,表现在土埂子上时,影子的长短会发生变化。夏天杆影最短的一天白天最长,叫作"日长至",也就是"夏至";冬天杆影最长的一天白天最短,叫作"日短至",也就是冬至;一年中,杆影长度适中有两次,就叫作春分或秋分。上述准确且简单的测量方法叫圭表测日影法,那根杆子称作"表",那条土埂子称作"土圭"。

中国最早装置圭表的观测台是西周初年(距今3 000多年)河南登封市告成镇的周公测景台。周公是西周初年著名的政治家、军事家,在天文地理方面也很有建树。他认为告成镇居于天下之中,所以在这里

周公测景台,底部石座是圭,上部石柱是表

Zhou Gong's Observatory, the lower stone seat is Gui, the upper stone pillar is table

rose to the middle of the sky, that is, to the south, the sun shined on the upright pole, whose projection fell on the north ridge. In winter and summer, the length of the shadow changed when the sun shined on the ridge. In summer, the pole shadow was the shortest while the day time was the longest. The day is called "the Solstice of Days", which was called "the Summer Solstice". In winter, the pole shadow was the longest while the day time was the shortest, which was called "Short Day Solstice" or "the Winter Solstice". In a year, the length of the shadow of a pole was moderate twice, which was called "the Spring Equinox" or "the Autumn Equinox". The above accurate and simple measurement method is called "the Gnomon Noon Shadow Measuring Method", the pole is called "Gnomon", and the ridge is called "Tugui".

The earliest observatory in China to install a gnomon was Zhou Gong Observatory in Gaocheng Town, Dengfeng City, Henan Province, in the early Western Zhou Dynasty (more than 3,000 years ago). Zhou Gong was a famous statesman and military strategist in the early Western Zhou Dynasty. He also made great achievements in astronomy and geography. He believed that Gaocheng Town was in the middle of the world, so he "piled up soil as the Gui, stood a pole as the table, measured noon shadows, found the middle of the world, set four seasons" here. Zhou Gong Observatory was used for coming generations. Stone poles were built in the Tang Dynasty. Guo Shoujing, an astronomer of the Yuan Dynasty, built a permanent observatory about 20 meters north of Zhou Gong Observatory, which improved the original Gui and pole. The length of ancient pole shadow rulers recorded in books before 1270 AD, is based on the length measured in Dengfeng Observatory in Henan Province.

In fact, as early as in the Shang Dynasty, people used this method to determine solar terms. The solar and monthly records in oracle bones inscriptions could be estimated in modern astronomical methods. The four solar terms of the Spring Equinox, the Autumn Equinox, the Summer Solstice and the Winter Solstice were used 3,000 years ago. They were developed to eight solar terms, namely the Beginning of Spring, the Spring Equinox, the Beginning of Summer, the Summer Solstice, the Beginning of Autumn, the Autumn Equinox, the Beginning of Winter, and the Winter Solstice in the Zhou Dynasty. These eight solar terms showed the seasonal change and clearly divided the four seasons of a year. With the need of production, the scope of observation was expanding and the observation time increased. By the time of the Qin and Han dynasties, the

"垒土为圭，立木为表，测日影，正地中，定四时"。周公测景台为以后几代所沿用。唐代时仿周公的土圭表在原址换成圭石表。元朝天文学家郭守敬在该测景台北约20米处建造了永久性的观星台，对原有的圭、表进行了改进。我们今天所能看到的公元1270年以前的书籍记载的古代杆影古尺长度均以河南登封测景台所测尺寸为准。

其实，早在商朝时，人们就用此法测定节气，甲骨文中的日月记录，用现代天文法推算，可以看到3 000年前已有春分、秋分、夏至和冬至四时的使用。周朝时发展到八个节气，即立春、春分、立夏、夏至、立秋、秋分、立冬、冬至。这八个节气表示出季节转换，清楚地划分出一年四季。随着劳动生产的需要，观察范围不断扩大，观察时间不断增加，到秦汉时期，二十四节气已基本完善，公元前132年《淮南子》一书中就完整记载了二十四节气的名称；公元前104年，汉武帝颁布《太初历》，正式把二十四节气编入历法，明确了二十四节气的天

元朝郭守敬在河南登封建的观星台
The Dengfeng Observatory in Henan Province which was built by Guo Shoujing in the Yuan Dynasty

twenty-four solar terms had been basically perfected. The names of the twenty-four solar terms were recorded in the book *Huainan Zi* in 132 BC. Emperor Wu of the Han Dynasty promulgated the *Taichu Calendar* in 104 BC, which formally included twenty-four solar terms in the calendar with their astronomical position clearly defined. Starting from the zero degree of the ecliptic longitude, the period of 15 degrees along the ecliptic longitude is called one solar term. The sun experiences twenty-four solar terms in a solar year, corresponding to 2 solar terms per calendar month. Among them, the first solar term of each month is called "season", namely, the Beginning of Spring, Awakening of Insects, Qingming, Beginning of Summer, Grain in Ear, Slight Heat, Beginning of Autumn, White Dew, Cold Dew, Beginning of Winter, Heavy Snow and Lesser Cold; the second solar term of each month is called "mid solar term", that is, Rain Water, Spring Equinox, Grain Rain, Lesser Fullness, Beginning of Summer, Great Heat, End of Heat, Autumn Equinox, Frosts Descent, Light Snow, Winter Solstice and Great Cold. "Season" and "mid solar term" alternately appeared, each lasting 15 days, collectively known as "solar terms".

    The twenty-four solar terms is the essence of Chinese traditional agricultural culture, which has been used for more than 2,000 years, guiding and influencing Chinese people's basic necessities of life. Each of their names is very scientific and aptly described in terms of solar terms or related to agriculture. For example, Qing Ming Festival originated from "All things grow in the world this time, the air is clean and the day is bright, thus this time is called Qing Ming". Lesser Fullness means that the seeds from the grain are becoming full but are not ripe. White Dew indicates the real beginning of cool autumn. The temperature declines gradually and the vapors in the air often condense into water-drops. These white water-drops adhere to flowers, grass and trees at night. When the morning comes, sunshine makes them look crystal clear, spotless white and adorable. Therefore, it is called White Dew.

    The twenty-four solar terms reflect the natural seasonal phenological characteristics of the middle and lower reaches of the Yellow River, including the whole Henan and parts of Shaanxi, Shanxi and Shandong provinces. China is a vast country in size and people express the same solar term in different places with different characteristics of the same solar term. Therefore, there are corresponding proverbs for agricultural production. In the long-term production and living practice, people, using the rhythm of poetry, compiled the solar terms into a song according to the order of the twenty-four solar terms, which has been chanted by

文位置。从太阳黄道经度0度开始，沿黄道经度每运行15度所经历的时日称为"一个节气"，太阳一个回归年共经历24个节气，每个公历月对应2个节气。其中，每月第一个节气称作"节令"，即立春、惊蛰、清明、立夏、芒种、小暑、立秋、白露、寒露、立冬、大雪和小寒；每月的第二个节气称作"中气"，即雨水、春分、谷雨、小满、夏至、大暑、处暑、秋分、霜降、小雪、冬至和大寒。"节令"和"中气"交替出现，各历时15天，统称为"节气"。

二十四节气是中国传统农业文化中的精华，至今已沿用了2 000多年，指导和影响着中国人的衣食住行。每一个节气的名字都非常科学而恰当地形容了需要定论的节气物候或与农业有关的事物，如清明节源自"世间万物生长此时，皆清洁而明净，故谓之清明"；小满，是指麦类夏熟作物灌浆乳熟，籽粒开始成熟，还没有达到完全饱满，所以叫小满；白露是指秋天空气中的水汽夜间成露，清晨在植物表面冷凝而呈白色，故名白露。

二十四节气反映的是黄河中下游，包括河南全部以及陕西、山西、山东部分地区的自然季节物候特征。中国幅员辽阔，同一节气各地都有自己的特点。在长期生产和生活实践中，人们还运用诗词韵律，按照二十四节气顺序，编了节气歌，一代又一代口口相传，无论长幼都会吟诵：

春雨惊春清谷天，夏满芒夏暑相连。

秋处露秋寒霜降，冬雪雪冬小大寒。

上半年逢六廿一，下半年逢八廿三。

每月两节不变更，最多相差一两天。

2016年11月30日，二十四节气被正式列入联合国教科文组织人类非物质文化遗产代表作名录。在国际气象界，二十四节气被誉为"中国的第五大发明"。

the old and the young, thus passing it down orally from generation to generation.

Spring begins before the rain, awakening of insects is followed by vernal equinox, clear and bright is the grain rain, summer begins before lesser fullness of grain, grain in ear is followed by summer solstice.

Slight heat and great heat come in a chain.

Autumn begins before the end of heat, white dews are followed by autumn equinox, cold dews come before hoar-frost falls, winter begins before the light snow falls, greater snow is followed by winter solstice, slight cold and great cold come in a row.

In the first half of the year the solar terms fall on the 6th and 21st days of each month, while in the second half of the year they fall usually on the 8th and 23rd days, it has never changed that 2 terms appear in each month, with at most one or two days in difference.

On November 30, 2016, the twenty-four solar terms were officially listed in the UNESCO list of representatives of intangible cultural heritage of mankind. In the world of meteorology, the twenty-four solar terms are known as the "fifth invention of China".

Ⅵ. Exquisite Brick and Stone Portraits in the Han Dynasty

The Western Han Dynasty and Eastern Han Dynasty were a period of prosperity in Chinese history. The main reason was that in the early Western Han Dynasty, the policy of "recuperation, subsistence and development of production" was implemented. In addition, the popularization and application of iron farming tools and farming techniques in agricultural production improved greatly the social productivity of the Han Dynasty. History books recorded that during 70 years from the beginning of the Western Han Dynasty to Emperor Wu's accession to the throne, there was no major disturbance in the country. If there were no floods or droughts, the people would always give their families enough food. The government's granaries were full of grain, and the state's coffers were full. In the capital, there were hundreds of millions of copper coins, even the strings of copper coins were rotted so that it was impossible to count how many they were. The grain in Taicang Granary accumulated year by year and overflowed outside, which were rotten and inedible. The social wealth was abundant, which provided favorable conditions for the creation of culture and art. Masonry tombs

六、汉代农耕"纪录片"——精美的汉画像砖石

两汉时期是中国历史上一个繁荣强盛的时期,主要原因是汉代初期实行了"休养生息"的政策,加上铁农具和农耕技术在农业生产上的推广应用,使得汉代的社会生产力获得了极大提高。史书上说,从汉朝初年到汉武帝即位的70年间,国家没有发生大的动乱。如果没有遇上旱涝灾害,百姓就总是家给人足,政府的粮仓装满粮食,国库的金钱有了多余。京城的钱积累到了千百万,连串钱的绳子都朽烂了,以致无法计数。太仓的粟米一年一年堆积,已经溢到了外面,腐烂不能食用。社会财富极大丰富,给文化艺术的创造提供了有利条件,厚葬尚饰的画像砖石墓因此流行开来。

画像砖石是指艺术家用模具模印烧制内容丰富、纹饰精美的画像砖,或以刀代笔,在坚硬的石面上创作精美的图像,用以作为建筑构件,起装饰作用。汉代砖石画像多是附在建筑墓穴壁面和楣楹碑阙上的装饰性艺术品。汉代画像砖石图像,涉及的题材非常广泛,包括了汉代社会生活的各个方面。单说农业生产活动的场面,如农耕纺织、渔猎采集、收获加工等场面,大多以写实的艺术手法表现,刻画得栩栩如生,就像纪录片一样生动真实地再现了汉代农业生产力水平及其发展演变的规律。

安徽滁州(属中原地区)出土的汉画像石拓片"田间劳作"
Farming scene of field work, a rubbing of the stone portrait of Han Dynasty, unearthed in Chuzhou, Anhui Province

with heavy burials and decorations were popular.

The brick and stone portraits refer to exquisite images on the brick or stone surface created by the artists who used molds to print and burn portrait bricks with rich decorative contents, or carved by the artisis, which could be used as building components for the purpose of decoration. Most of the brick and stone portraits in the Han Dynasty were decorative works of art attached to the walls of architectural tombs and the lintel tablets. The images of brick and stone portraits in the Han Dynasty covered a wide range of subjects, including all aspects of social life in the Han Dynasty. The scenes of agricultural production activities, such as farming, spinning and weaving, fishing, hunting, harvesting and processing, were mostly depicted by realistic artistic techniques. They vividly and truly reproduced the level of agricultural productivity, the law of the development and evolution in the Han Dynasty, just like documentaries.

The masonry tombs of the Han Dynasty were located in the middle and lower reaches of the Yellow River, Sichuan and Jiangsu provinces, where the bureaucrats and rich people of the Han Dynasty gathered together, and where agriculture, industry and commerce and social economy were most developed. The themes of the tomb portraits also had regional characteristics. For example, there were many textile and farming scenes in the portraits of Shandong Province and Jiangsu Province, there were many farmland reclamation and grazing areas in Shaanxi Province, there were more scenes reflecting southern paddy farming in Sichuan Province. The portraits of Henan region more reflected the scenes of officials and rich people enjoying delicious food with music and hunting leisurely.

From unearthed portraits of the Han Dynasty, the popular farming method was to use two-cattle-and-one-man. At that time, the plough had been basically finalized and had the main parts of the modern one. The original plough was to connect the shoulders of two cattle with a wooden bar, and a vertical bar was tied between the poles to connect the plough. The aim was to get the two cattle to pull a plough together, which was called the "two cattle lifting bar". People constantly thought how to exert more cow power. In the Eastern Han Dynasty, one cattle-pulled plough appeared. It was easy to cultivate on small farmland. It was more advanced and more efficient than the commonly used "two cattle ploughing". In today's remote mountainous areas of China, especially on steep and small hillside arable land, a cattle pulling a plough can be occasionally seen. In the sunset, accompanied by the farmers' yelling, the brown soil rolls under the plough. What

汉代画像砖石墓遍及黄河中下游地区以及四川、江苏等地，这些地方都是汉代官僚富豪云集，农业、工商业和社会经济最发达的地区，墓葬画像题材也具有区域特征。比如，山东、江苏画像中纺织、耕作场面多，陕西垦田、放牧场面多，西南部的四川则有较多反映南方水田农作的场面。河南地区农业生产在全国居领先地位，作为政治经济文化中心，河南地区的画像更多地反映官僚富贾钟鸣鼎食、悠闲游猎的场面。

从各地出土的画像看，汉代牛耕普遍采用二牛一人的耕作方法。当时的耕犁已经基本定型，具有了现代犁的主要部件。最初的犁是用一根木杠把两头牛的肩连接起来，木杠中间又系一竖杠与犁连接，目的是让两头牛合力去拉动一张犁耕地，这就是所谓的"二牛抬杠"式。人们不断地琢磨如何更大地发挥牛的力量，到东汉时就出现了"一牛挽犁"的耕作形式，便于在小块农田上耕作，比普遍使用的"二牛抬杠"更进步，效率更高。在中国一些偏远山区，尤其是又陡又小的山坡耕地上，我们偶尔还能看到"一牛挽犁"的身影，夕阳西下，伴着农人的吆喝

安徽徐州出土的汉画像拓片"二牛抬杠"
Two cattle lifting bar, the rubbing of the stone portait of Han Dynasty, unearthed in Xuzhou, Anhui Province

陕西绥德西山寺出土的汉画像拓片"一牛挽犁"
One cattle ploughing, the rubbing of the stone portait of Han Dynasty, unearthed in Xishan Temple, Shaanxi Province

a unique poetic scene!

The popularization of cattle farming has promoted the progress of land preparation technology. The field management of crops reflected the advanced farming technology in the Han Dynasty. The intertillage is an important part of intensive farming. A portrait of intertillage stone was unearthed in Nanyang City, Henan Province. In the waist-deep field of crops, a peasant wearing a pointed cap with a long-handled hoe in hand is weeding and heaping soil for crops. The peasant's wife is at the right end, with her hair tied, dressed in a brooch skirt, carrying a triangular hoe on her shoulder, with a water jar at the end of the hoe handle and a basket at the other end of the hoe. She is calling the peasant to have a meal and preparing to take his place. The waist-deep crops in the field should be the popular millet in the Han Dynasty. There is a deer running on the edge of the ground, which symbolizes auspiciousness to pray for a good weather and to hope for a good harvest.

Peasants in the Han Dynasty attached great importance to fertilization to improve soil. The application of organic fertilizer has promoted the biological cycle and made the soil fertile.

Crops reflected in the brick and stone portraits of the Han Dynasty were millet, rice, wheat, beans, taro and lotus root, which constituted the basic source of staple food. The emergence of stone mills led to a rapid increase in the proportion of wheat, wheat became the most common staple food of the northern people in the Han Dynasty. It was from this time that the northerners began to like pasta.

Many stone portraits also showed the vastness of camel fleets in the Western Regions. They traveled long distance to China along the miraculous Silk Road. They not only brought the customs of the Western Regions, but also rare flowers and grasses that the Han people had never seen, such as grapes, pomegranates, alfalfa, safflower, jute, walnuts, courgettes, garlic and onions, which were introduced into Central Plains at that time.

Ⅷ. Ancient Chinese Agricultural Encyclopedia *Qimin Yaoshu*

In the first half of the sixth century AD, Jia Sixie, a native of Qingzhou, Shandong Province, was an official travelling frequently far from his hometown. When he was official in places like Henan and Hebei, and was able to inspect

河南南阳出土的中耕画像石
The portrait of intertillage stone, unearthed in Nanyang City, Henan Province

声，褐色的土在犁铧下翻滚，别有一番诗意。

牛耕的普及，推动了整地技术的进步。汉代先进的耕作技术，还体现在对农作物的田间管理上。中耕是精耕细作农业重要的组成部分。河南南阳出土了一块中耕画像石，在长满齐腰深庄稼的地里，一个农夫头戴尖顶帽，手持长柄锄正在为庄稼除草壅土。右端刻一个农妇，梳着发髻，穿着襦裙，肩扛一把三角形锄，锄柄端系一个水罐，锄根部挂一个篮子，她正在招呼锄地的男子喝水用饭，并准备替换劳作。田间齐腰深的庄稼从形态上看，应为汉代流行种植的粟。地边有一只象征祥瑞的奔鹿，意在祈祷风调雨顺，期盼五谷丰登。

汉代农家非常重视施肥以改良土壤，用地与养地相结合，施用有机肥促进了自然界生物循环，使地力肥沃。

汉代砖石画像上反映的农作物大体上有粟、黍、稻、麦、豆、芋、藕等，这些农作物构成汉代人主食的基本来源。石磨的出现导致麦在五谷中种植比重迅速上升，麦成为汉代北方人最普遍的主食，北方人喜爱面食就是从这个时候开始的。

有不少画像石还表现了西域诸国的驼队浩浩荡荡，沿着丝绸之路，长途跋涉来到中国，他们不仅带来了西域风情，还带来了汉人从来没有听说过的奇花异草，葡萄、石榴、苜蓿、红蓝花、胡麻、胡桃、胡瓜、

many places in the middle and lower reaches of the Yellow River. On the basis of thorough investigation, he wrote the book *Qimin Yaoshu*, summarizing the experience and innovative ideas of the development of agriculture in these areas before the sixth century AD. The book, with totaling 110,000 words, and known as the "Ancient Chinese Agricultural Encyclopedia", is one of the earliest monographs in the history of agriculture in the world. It is also the earliest and most complete ancient comprehensive agricultural book in China.

Well-structured with a clear sequence of ideas, comprehensive elaboration from land reclamation to cultivation, from pre-production preparation to post-production agricultural product processing, brewing and utilization, from planting, forestry to livestock and poultry breeding, and to aquaculture industry, *Qimin Yaoshu* has established a relatively complete agricultural system. It incisively reveals the key points of dryland agricultural technology in the middle and lower reaches of the Yellow River, emphasizing that the technical links such as tilling, harrowing, raking, pressing, ploughing, drilling, and hoeing should be skillfully coordinate. It also presents many important innovative ideas in soil transformation, crop rotation, green manure planting, field layout, and winter irrigation. *Qimin Yaoshu*, which attaches importance to comprehensive analysis of agricultural production, science and technology, and economic benefits, has pushed the dryland farming technology in the middle and lower reaches of the Yellow River to a higher level. In short, *Qimin Yaoshu*, a masterpiece of science and technology, has been in circulation for about 1,500 years, and the subsequent four large-scale agricultural books, *Nongsang Jiyao* (*Excerpts on Farming and Sericulture*), *Wang Zhen Nongshu* (*Wang Zhen's Agricultural Book*), *Nongzheng Quanshu* (*A Complete Book on Agricultural Administration*), *Shoushi Tongkao* (*Excerpts on Farming*) had all followed the example of it. So far, it is still regarded as a classic work of ancient farming books.

However, Jia Sixie's writing of *Qimin Yaoshu* is far from writing a farming book. He had been an official in his lifetime, and deeply realized that agricultural production was not only a necessary condition for life, but also a foundation of peace and stability for governing the country. Food is the paramount necessity of the people. With food there are people, with people there is the society, and with a society there are officials. So officials must regard it as their own responsibility.

How do the later generations evaluate *Qimin Yaoshu*?

Agronomists say that it has enabled Chinese agronomy to form a complete

胡蒜、胡葱等都是那时传入并在中原安家的。

七、中国古代农业百科全书《齐民要术》

公元6世纪上半叶，山东青州人贾思勰辗转在远离家乡的外地做官，他游宦到河南、河北等地，也因此得以考察黄河中下游的许多地方，在充分调研的基础上撰写了《齐民要术》一书，总结了6世纪以前黄河中下游地区农业发展的经验与创新思路。全书共11万字，被誉为"中国古代农业百科全书"，堪称世界农学史上最早的专著之一，也是中国现存最早、最完整的古代综合性农书。

《齐民要术》全书结构严谨，从开荒到耕种，从生产前的准备到生产后的农产品加工、酿造与利用，从种植业、林业到畜禽饲养业、水产养殖业，论述全面，脉络清楚，为较为完整的农学体系的建立打下了基础，精辟透彻地揭示了黄河中下游旱地农业技术的关键所在，强调耕、耙、耱、压、犁、耧、锄等技术环节的巧妙配合；在土壤改造、作物轮作换茬、绿肥种植翻压、田间布局与冬灌等方面，有许多重要创见。

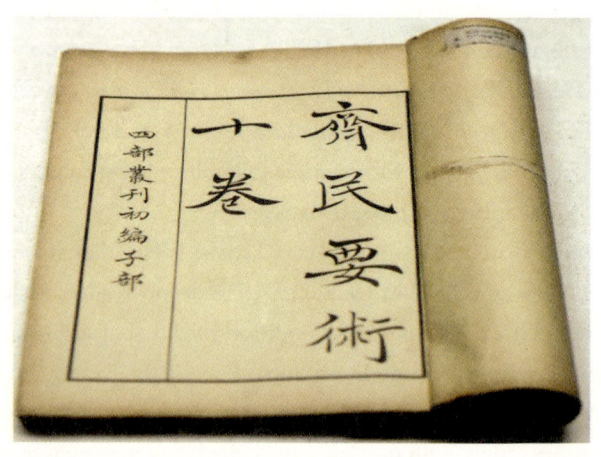

《齐民要术》民间收藏本
Qimin Yaoshu, a private collection

structural system of intensive farming for the first time, which has led to a deeper development of agriculture.

Politicians say that it is "the politics of benefiting the people, and the art of training farmers and enriching the country".

Economic historians say that it serves as a management guide for the feudal landlord economy, which provides a favorable way to increase economic benefit.

Food historians say it is " an Ancient Chinese Cooking Encyclopedia".

Darwin's *The Origin of Species* refers to it as "the Ancient Chinese Encyclopedia".

Ⅷ. The Great Development of Agriculture in the Sui, Tang and Song Dynasties

At the end of the sixth century AD, the splitting and separating situation of China eventually came to an end, ushering in a great unification. Henan was one of the food supply bases to the capital in the early years of the Sui Dynasty. However, the Sui Dynasty was a short-lived dynasty. In the early 7th century AD (in 618 AD), a great prosperous dynasty, the Tang Dynasty, was born with a very vast territory, as large as 12.37 million square kilometers in its prime (one version says it was 10.76 million square kilometers). It was also an important period of the fastest economic development in the history of China.

In the early Tang Dynasty, the issuance of The Act of Average Allocation and The Zuyongdiao System (paying rent with grain in place of cloth) had greatly pushed forward the economic recovery and development. In particular, the construction of water conservancy projects in Henan had promoted the agricultural development. The poem *Recalling the Past* by Du Fu, a poet of the Tang Dynasty, known as the Sage of Chinese Poetry, depicts the prosperous days in the Kaiyuan Periods of the Tang Dynasty as:

In reminiscence of the good old days of the flourishing Kaiyuan Period, even a small city may house over ten thousands of residents.

A good harvest comes with abundant rice and white millet, with which the public and private warehouses are filled.

With no robbers or thieves in the roads throughout the country, one does not have to await a white day to go on a long journey.

Commercial carts full of white and fine silk from Qi and Lu come and go, and

《齐民要术》把黄河中下游旱地农耕技术推向了较高的水平，并重视对农业生产、科学技术与经济效益进行综合分析。总之，作为一部科学技术名著，《齐民要术》流传了约1 500年的时间，此后的四部大型农书《农桑辑要》《王祯农书》《农政全书》《授时通考》均取法于《齐民要术》。至今，《齐民要术》仍被人们奉作古农书的经典著作。

但贾思勰撰写《齐民要术》远非写一本农书而已。他一生为官，深刻认识到农业生产既是生活所必需，也是治国安民的根本，因为民以食为天，有食才有民，有民才有社会，有社会才有官，所以为官者必须以"食为政首"为己任。

后世是怎么评价《齐民要术》的呢？

农学家说它使中国农学第一次形成精耕细作的完整的结构体系，使农业向纵深发展。

政治家说它是"惠民之政，训农裕国之术"。

经济史学家说它是封建地主经济的经营指南，为增加经济效益提供了有利的途径。

食品史学家说它是"中国古代的烹饪百科全书"。

达尔文的《物种起源》中说它是"中国古代百科全书"。

八、隋唐宋农业大发展

公元6世纪末，中国分裂割据的局面终于结束，迎来了大一统。河南在隋朝初年是京都粮食供应基地之一。但是隋朝是个短命的王朝，公元7世纪初（618年），一个伟大的盛世朝代——唐朝诞生，它的疆域十分辽阔，疆域面积最大时达1 237万平方公里（一说1 076万平方公里），也是中国历史上经济发展最快的时期。

唐初颁布均田令和租庸调（以粮食代替布匹缴租）后，经济得以大大恢复和发展，特别是河南境内诸多地区兴建水利工程，促进了农业

men working in the fields with women weaving at home give a sign of stability.

This poem vividly reflects the prosperity of the Tang Dynasty during the Kaiyuan period. Although there are effusive elements in it, it should be basically in line with the historical reality, as there was no reason for fabrication.

In the Tang and Song dynasties, the agricultural structure mainly consisted of grain, silkworm, mulberry, cotton and hemp, animal husbandry, horticulture (fruit trees, vegetables, flowers, medicinal materials, tea, etc.) and forestry. However, it is still dominated by "farming and sericulture" by which cereals and clothing materials are produced. Since the Neolithic Age the grain structure in China had been dominated by millet and rice, as the saying goes, "Millet is produced in the north and rice in the south". By the time of the Song Dynasty, rice and wheat had taken the first place. In the middle of the 10th century, Henan was one of the areas where rice was rapidly popularized. At that time, there was a special rice farming organization called "the Rice Field Affairs Office". Baiquan Town of Weihui City, with abundant water resources and excellent water quality, used to produce rice which became a tribute to the royal court. With highly advanced technology in production of tea, wood, flowers and vegetables, many southern fruits such as alfalfa, camellia and figs had been successfully planted in the north, indicating that the technology of transplanting southern plants to the Central Plains was mature. In addition, the grafting technology at that time was very mature.

In the Tang Dynasty, the ploughing tool was changed from a straight plough to a curved one, which was a major achievement in the history of plough, and the Chinese plough was thus shaped. In addition, a variety of tools, compatible with the curved plough, had been developed. Water mills were used for grain processing. The Chinese noria appeared as the irrigation tool.

In the Sui, Tang and Northern Song dynasties, Henan's economy and culture reached the peak in history, and it was also a period of great development of water conservancy. The Grand Canal was excavated to form the Grand Canal system with Luoyang of Henan as the center, connecting the South and the North. Irrigation was developed in Henan, and many farmland water conservancy projects were restored. Large areas of saline-alkali land had been improved by silt irrigation and siltation in the middle and lower reaches of the Yellow River.

发展。被誉为中国"诗圣"的唐朝诗人杜甫的诗《忆昔》描写了开元盛世的景象:"忆昔开元全盛日,小邑犹藏万家室。稻米流脂粟米白,公私仓廪俱丰实。九州道路无豺虎,远行不劳吉日出。齐纨鲁缟车班班,男耕女桑不相失。"这首诗形象地反映了唐朝开元年间的富足景象。当然,诗与历史并不完全相同,这里不免有溢美之词,但基本合乎历史实际,因为艺术源于生活。

唐宋时期农业结构主要由谷物、蚕桑棉麻、畜牧、园艺(果树、蔬菜、花卉、药材、茶叶)、林木等组成,但仍然以谷物和"农桑"为主。中国农作物结构自新石器时代起,就以粟稻为主,人们常说"北粟南稻"。到宋朝时,稻麦已占首位。10世纪中期,河南是水稻推广种植较发达的地区之一,当时出现了专门的种植水稻的农耕组织"稻田务"。卫辉市百泉水源丰富,水质极佳,所产稻米成了贡品。茶、林木、花卉、蔬菜等都非常普遍,枇杷、山茶、无花果等许多南方水果在北方成功种植,说明将南方植物移植中原的技术已经成熟。当时的嫁接技术也已十分成熟。

唐时,犁地工具由直辕犁变成曲辕犁,这是耕犁史上的重大成就,中国耕犁就此定型。此外还出现了与耕犁相配套的各种工具。粮食加

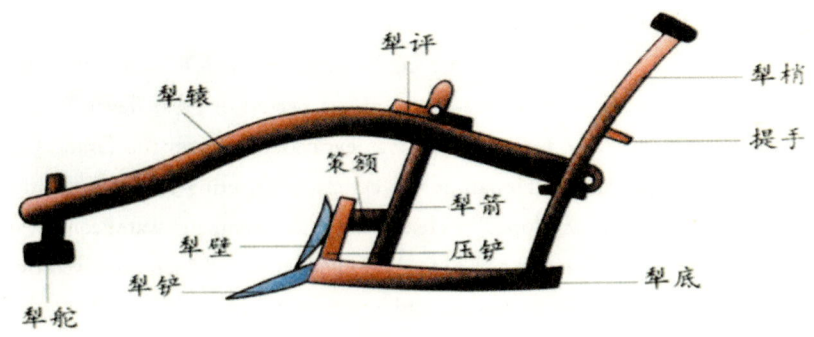

唐朝曲辕犁
Quyuan Plow in the Tang Dynasty

IX. Henan Agriculture in the Yuan, Ming and Qing Dynasties

During the Yuan, Ming and Qing dynasties, the development of agriculture in Henan gradually slowed down due to the shift of economic center to the south and political center to the north. During this period, Henan agriculture presented the following characteristics: agronomic theory was more mature and agricultural books increased in number. The agricultural and social structures were becoming more rational and gradually shaped. Although the focus of economic development had shifted southward and the political situation was turbulent, Henan remained one of the important agricultural production bases in the country until the Ming and Qing dynasties.

In the early Yuan Dynasty, the government advocated the policy of "taking full advantage of the land", which encouraged stationing and reclamation of wasteland, and expanding communications between the north and the south; and therefore promoted the development of the agricultural economy and made significant advancements of science and technology. The three famous agricultural books in the Yuan Dynasty, *Nongsang Jiyao* (*Fundamentals of Agriculture and Sericulture*), *Wang Zhen Nongshu* (*Wang Zhen's Agricultural Book*), *Nongsang Yishi Cuoyao* (*Summary of Farming, Sericulture, Clothing and Food*) are all agricultural books which take both the North and the South into account, attach equal importance to agriculture and sericulture, and focus on the introduction of agricultural science and technology. In particular, the book *Nongsang Jiyao*, systematically summarizes the experience of farming technology before the 13th century. It is the earliest existing official agricultural book in China, whose influences reach far beyond China. At the beginning of the Yuan Dynasty, the farmers' department was set up to take charge of agriculture, sericulture and water conservancy. The famous water conservancy project Guangji Canal was built in Henan to irrigate the farmland with water from the Qinhe River. Due to good water conservancy conditions, more than 700 hectares of wasteland were reclaimed in just one year. In Henan,"population increases gradually", "villagers are living in peace, and the wild is covered with mulberry trees and hemp", which manifest the initial signs of prosperity.

During the Ming and Qing dynasties, more attention was paid to making full

工,利用水碾或水磨。灌溉工具出现了筒车。

隋、唐、北宋时期,河南经济文化达到历史上的鼎盛阶段,也是水利大发展的时期。大运河的开凿,形成了以河南洛阳为中心的连接南北的大运河系统。河南大力发展灌溉,修复了许多农田水利工程。黄河中下游引浊灌淤,改良了大片盐碱地。

九、重视技术、多熟种植——元明清时期的河南农业

元明清时,由于经济重心南移,政治中心北移,河南农业发展速度逐渐下降。这一时期河南农业呈现出如下特点:农学理论更加成熟,农书增加;农业结构和社会结构日趋合理并逐渐定型;虽然经济发展重心南移,政局动荡不安,但直到明清时期河南仍是全国的重要农业生产基地之一。

元朝初年,政府提倡"地利毕兴",鼓励屯垦,扩大南北交流,因此,促进了农业经济的发展。农业科学技术有明显进步,著名的元代三部农书——《农桑辑要》《王祯农书》《农桑衣食撮要》,都是南北兼顾、农桑并重,着重总结农业科技知识的农书。《农桑辑要》对13世纪以前的农耕技术经验作了系统总结和研究。该书是中国现存最早的官修农书,影响远及国外。元初还设立了劝农司,专掌农桑水利。河南境内修筑了著名的水利工程广济渠,引沁河水灌溉农田。由于水利条件好,一年就垦荒700余顷。河南地区"民日生集","烟火相望,桑麻被野",初露繁荣景象。

明清时,政府更加注重充分利用土地和提高土地生产效率,因而这一时期的农业经营朝着集约化方向发展。主要措施之一是大力推行多熟种植,黄河流域普遍形成了二年三熟或三年四熟制。耕作制度呈多样化和复杂化特点,精耕细作程度加深,套犁深耕、浅耕灭茬、沙田栽培、看苗施肥、小麦移栽等技术大多形成或完善于这一时期。栽培、灌溉、

use of the land and improving the productivity of land. As a result, agricultural operations in the Ming and Qing dynasties developed towards intensification. One of the main measures was to vigorously practice the multi-ripening planting, and the system of three ripenings in two years or four ripenings in three years generally took shape in the Yellow River Basin. The tillage system was diversified and complicated. More intensive cultivation techniques like deep ploughing tillage, shallow ploughing for stubble eradication, sand cultivation, pro-field method, seedling fertilization, and wheat transplanting were formed or perfected during this period. Techniques such as cultivation, irrigation, fertilization, and control of diseases and pests were rapidly developed. In order to make full use of the land, a diversified management of artificial ecological agriculture was practiced in some areas, such as the combination of grain, animal husbandry, mulberry and fishery.

Due to the increasing intensification of agricultural products, specialized production of certain produce appeared in some areas, such as the specialized cotton-producing areas in Henan and Shandong. During the Ming and Qing dynasties, handicrafts such as textiles, brewing, tobacco making and sugar refining developed rapidly, and the towns became increasingly prosperous. The demand for agricultural products grew rapidly, and the planting scale of economic crops increased quickly as well.

In the Ming and Qing dynasties, quite a number of new crops, such as corn, sweet potato, potato, peanut, tomato, cabbage, onion, sunflower, cauliflower, sugar beet and tobacco, were introduced into the Central Plains, through the Maritime Silk Road, all of which can be planted throughout Henan Province. Ever since the 19th century, corn, sweet potato, potato and other crops had partially replaced the traditional crops such as broomcorn and millet. These crops, mostly featured by high yield, and high adaptability, had greatly alleviated the situation of food shortage at the time, and increased the utilization rate of barren land, thus, making important contribution to meeting the needs of a rapidly growing population after they were commonly planted. During the Ming and Qing dynasties, China also made great achievements in animal husbandry and forestry, including the cultivation of many famous animal breeds, extensive advocating of tree planting and forestry cultivation. Further research had been done on technologies concerning the direct seeding of economic forests, cutting grafting, and seedling cultivation.

Another two important agricultural books are worth mentioning. One is *Nongzheng Quanshu (A Complete Book on Agricultural Administration)*,

施肥和病虫害防治等技术得以迅速发展。为了充分利用土地，有些地区实行了多种经营为一体的人工生态农业，如粮、牧、桑、渔互养。

由于农作物产品化程度越来越高，有些地区出现了某类农产品的专业生产，例如河南、山东等地出现专业产棉区。明清时，纺织、酿造、制烟、制糖等手工业迅速发展，城镇日渐繁荣，对农产品的需求日增，其他经济作物的种植规模也迅速发展起来。

明清时期，玉米、甘薯、马铃薯、花生、番茄、包白、洋葱、向日葵、花菜、甜菜和烟草等农业新作物通过海上丝绸之路得以引进并在中原推广，河南全境都可以种植。自19世纪起，玉米、甘薯、马铃薯等作物已部分取代黍、稷等传统作物。因这些作物大多具有高产、适应性强等特点，得以普遍种植，大大改善了粮食不够吃的状况，同时也提高了贫瘠土地的利用率，为满足快速增长的人口的粮食需求做出了重要贡献。明清时期，我国畜牧业和林业方面也取得了不少成就，培育出了很多著名畜种，植树育林被广为提倡，对经济林木直播与插条嫁接及育苗技术的研究更加深入。

还有两部重要的农书，一部是明代著名科学家、政治家徐光启（1562—1633）编撰的《农政全书》，这本书囊括了中国明代农业生产和人民生活的各个方面，见解独到，内容丰富，在农业类古书中空前绝后，而且全书表达了治国治民的"农政"思想。另一部是明末清初科学家宋应星（1587—1666）编撰的《天工开物》，全书对各种农作物和手工业原料的种类、产地、生产技术和工艺装备等进行了系统总结，构成了一个完整的科学技术体系。书中记述的"物种发展变异理论"和"动物杂交培育良种"技术比德国和法国的早一二百年，尤其是"骨灰蘸秧根""种性随水土而分"等研究成果，更是农业史上的重大突破。

compiled by Xu Guangqi (1562-1633), a famous scientist and statesman of the Ming Dynasty. With the author's unique insights and experiences, this unprecedented book covers all aspects of agricultural production and people's life in the Ming Dynasty of China. And the ideas of "agricultural politics" for governing the country and the people can be perceived throughout the book. The other is *Tiangong Kaiwu* (*Chinese Technology in the Seventeenth Century*), compiled by the scientist Song Yingxing (1587-1666) in the late Ming and early Qing dynasties. The book systematically summarizes various crops and the raw materials, production areas, production techniques and processes, and the equipment of the handicraft industry. The "theories on species development and variation" and "animal hybrid breeding technology" described in the book are one or two hundred years earlier than those recorded in Germany and France. In particular, the research achievements such as "dipping the seedling roots with bone ashes" and "the species division by soil and water" could be called the major breakthroughs in the history of agriculture.

X. The "Idea of Three Vitals" in Agricultural Production Practice

Most of the primary school students in China can recite *San Zi Jing* (*Three-Character Classics*), in which there are such words, Three Vitals mean heaven, earth, and man. Heaven, earth and man, are called Three Vitals by the ancient people. The knowledge of the relationship and interaction among the three has been gradually deepened in the course of China's traditional agricultural development.

As early as in the pre-Qin Period of China, more than 3,000 years ago, the idea of taking Three Vitals into account in agricultural production had taken its initial form. The earliest discussion of the relationship among heaven, earth, and man in agriculture can be found in *Lüshi Chunqiu* (*Lü's Spring and Autumn Annals*), "Crops are sowed by man, germinated by the earth, and fostered by the heaven". This relationship is also described in the book *Xun Zi* (*The Book of Master Xun*) as the ability of man to cooperate with the heaven and the earth. "The heaven has its time, the earth has its wealth, and the man has its power. And this power enables people to stand as one of the three vitals." In short, in ancient times, heaven, earth and man were three important factors indispensable to agricultural production. As people continue to know more about the heaven, the

十、农业生产实践中的"三才思想"

中国的小学生大多都会背诵《三字经》,其中有"三才者,天地人"。天时、地利、人和,古人谓之"三才",三者相互作用的观念在中国传统农业发展历程中逐渐得以深化。

早在3 000多年前的中国先秦时期,农业要兼顾天、地、人的"三才思想"就已初步形成。最早论述农业生产中天、地、人关系的是《吕氏春秋》,"夫稼,为之者人也,生之者地也,养之者天也"。《荀子》中也说:"天有其时,地有其财,人有其治,夫是之谓能参。"总之,远古时期,天、地、人在农业生产中是不可或缺的三个重要因素。人们在农业生产中不断认识天和地,不断认识自我,天、地、人三者的关系在人们的意识中也不断发生着变化,发展历程大致经历了三个阶段。

第一阶段是先秦时期,社会生产力低下,靠天吃饭,人们认为天时具有决定性意义,风调雨顺,才能有好收成,"勿夺农时"是农业生产着重强调的。《夏小正》、二十四节气、七十二物候等都是为了让人们对天时有正确的认识,以便不误农时。

第二阶段是秦汉以后一直到唐宋时期的1 400多年间,农业生产中的"三才思想"发生了重要变化,即用天时、地财、人力的概念取代先秦时期的天时、地利、人和的概念。《淮南子》中说:"上因天时,下尽地财,中用人力,是以群生遂长,五谷蕃殖。"西汉文景时期,晁错也说:"粟米布帛,生于地,长于时,聚于力。""三才"的观念中,人的因素有"人和"到"人力"的演变,意味着要使人的主观因素和天时、地利等客观因素相配合,以适应自然。所以,《氾胜之书》(公元前1世纪)提出了"趋时、和土、务粪泽、早锄早获"的十一字农业耕种方针,主要强调的是要合理使用土地。《齐民要术》的指导思想是

earth, and themselves in agricultural production, their understanding of the three vitals has been constantly changing. These changes have roughly gone through the following three stages.

The first stage was the pre-Qin Period, when the social productivity was low and people depended on the weather for food. So people believed that weather was decisive for harvest and good harvest could be achieved only when the weather was favorable. "Do not let the farming time slip by" is particularly emphasized in agricultural production. *Xia Xiao Zheng*, the twenty-four solar terms, and the seventy-two phenological signs are all for people to have a correct understanding of the heavenly time, so as not to miss the time for farming.

The second stage was a period of over 1,400 years starting from the Qin Dynasty to the Song Dynasty, during which the concept of the "Idea of Three Vitals" in agricultural production underwent important changes. In other words, the concept of heavenly time, land wealth and human power had replaced the pre-Qin concept of the right time, the right place and the right people. *Huainan Zi (The Book of Master Huainan)* says that "the monarch is to adapt to the changes of the four seasons in heaven, to exert its potential as much as possible on the earth, and to use the power of the people in the country so that all things can grow smoothly and the crops can be reproduced". During the period of Emperor Wen and Emperor Jing of the Western Han Dynasty, Chao Cuo, one of the chief officials of the time, also said that "the corns and textiles are born in the ground, grown with time, and gathered with manpower". In the concept of "Three Vitals", the evolution of the human factor from the "human harmony" to "human power" means that the subjective factor of human beings should be matched with the objective factors such as the right time and the right place, and should adapt to the natural atmosphere. Therefore, *The Book by Fan Sheng* (1st century BC) puts forward the eleven-(Chinese) character agricultural cultivation policy, "Qu shi, he tu, wu fen ze, zao chu zao huo" which means "the essence of farming lies in following the season to increase the activity of the soil by applying the manure, and by hoeing in time for a good harvest", mainly emphasizing the rational use of land. The guiding principle of *Qimin Yaoshu* is that "it is more likely to gain success with less efforts by adapting to the right time and the right place, while it is likely to gain nothing even with hard work by going against the natural law", in which the respect for the right time is emphasized while measuring the right place reminds people of the possibility that their work may eventually come to

"顺天时，量地利，用力少而成功多，任情逆道，劳而无获"，其中也强调了对天时的尊重，"量地利"则告诫人们如果不关注地利，一样会劳而无获。

第三阶段是明清时期，"三才思想"继续深化，提出要积极发挥人的主观能动性。由于人多地少的矛盾日益突出，充分发挥人的能动作用就成为关键。明代丘濬在《大学衍义补》中说："土性虽有宜不宜，人力亦有至不至，人力之至，亦或可以回天。"这种把人作为核心的"天地人合一"的观念，奠定了中国以种植业为主导的精耕细作的传统农业的指导思想。

明清时期，因种种原因，中国农业未能向近代农业过渡，而是沿着原来的道路纵深发展，精耕细作的优良传统趋于定型。纵观农业发展史，古人用令人叹为观止的智慧建造出了宏大的水利工程，发明了先进的农业技术，今人应当取其精华，去其糟粕，学习古人智慧，并将其运用于当代。

nothing if these factors are ignored.

The third stage is the Ming and Qing dynasties when the "Idea of Three Vitals" was deepened and emphasizing the active exertion of the subjective initiative of human beings. Since the contradiction between people and land was becoming more and more prominent, it became a key issue to give full play to the active role of people. In the Ming Dynasty, Qiu Jun said in *Daxue Yanyi Bu* (*The Supplement of the Derivative Meaning of The Great Learning*), "The land may be or may not be suitable for farming, and the manpower may be or may not be strong enough for cultivation, however, when the manpower is strong enough, man is likely to win over the right time." This idea of taking man as the core factor of "the unity of heaven, earth and man" laid the foundation for the guiding principle for the traditional agriculture of intensive cultivation dominated by crop farming in China.

During the Ming and Qing dynasties, for various reasons, Chinese agriculture failed to make the transition to modern agriculture, but developed in depth along its original path. The fine tradition of intensive cultivation tended to be stereotyped. Throughout the history of agricultural development, the ancient people had built water conservancy projects and invented advanced agricultural technologies with their amazing wisdom. We should learn from the wisdom of the ancient people and apply it to modern agriculture.

第三章

质的飞越——河南现代农业

Chapter III

Modern Agriculture

传统农业毕竟是以农民世代使用的各种生产要素为基础的农业，传统农业自给自足的自然经济形式使得中国的经济在工业化的历史进程中渐渐落伍。中华人民共和国成立后，国家工业化战略的推进和社会主义市场经济体制的确立，标志着传统农业向现代农业的转向。2016年，中央一号文件提出加强资源保护和生态修复，推动农业绿色发展。改革开放40多年来，河南农业和农村经济发生了翻天覆地的变化。如今，河南省也正在尝试发展生态农业，统筹推进"布局区域化、经营规模化、生产标准化、发展产业化"，加快建设现代农业强省。河南现已成为全国小麦产量第一大省，全国花生产量第一大省，肉牛总数全国第一，奶牛总数全国第四。河南特色农产品资源丰富，其中，食用菌全国第一，中药材和蔬菜全国前三。大量农副产品走出河南、走向全国、走向世界，"中国粮仓""国人厨房""百姓餐桌"的美誉当之无愧。

一、中国人的"大粮仓"

2014年5月，习近平总书记在河南调研指导工作时明确指出，河南粮食生产这个优势、这张王牌，任何时候都不能丢。河南省106个县中有95个是产粮大县。在调整结构的大背景下，河南坚持"藏粮于地、藏粮于技"战略，建设高标准粮田，切实保障粮食综合生产能力，成为名副其实的国家粮食生产核心区。2004年以来，河南粮食产量实现了"十二连增"，连续跨越了900亿斤、1000亿斤、1100亿斤和1200亿斤四大台阶。河南用中国1/16 的土地生产了中国 1/10 的粮食，其中，小麦产量达到700亿斤，占中国的27%。

2014年以来，河南大力推进农业供给侧结构性改革，重点发展"优质小麦、优质花生、优质草畜、优质果蔬"，调整农业结构。河南这个"大粮仓"不仅粮食富足，还生产了充足的肉蛋奶。河南牛的饲养量为1 400万头，居中国第一；猪 1 亿头，居中国第二；家禽 16 亿只，居

Traditional agriculture is based on various production factors employed by farmers from generation to generation, of which self-sufficient economy made Chinese economy fall behind in the process of industrialization. After the foundation of People's Republic of China, state industrialization strategy was promoted and socialist market economy established, which symbolized a change from traditional agriculture to modern one. In 2016, the "No. 1 Document of the CPC Central Committee" called for enforcing resources conservation and ecological remediation and promoting green development of agriculture. More than forty years' reform and opening-up has witnessed great changes in agriculture and rural economy of Henan which is endeavoring to develop eco-agriculture and promoting "regionalized distribution, scaled-up operations, standardized production and industrialized development" in order to accelerate the construction of a great province in modern agriculture. Nowadays, Henan has already become the largest producer for wheat, peanut and beef cattle in China and the fourth largest producer for dairy cows. Moreover, it enjoys rich resources of distinctive agricultural products, among which edible fungi rank the first in China and Chinese herbal medicines and vegetables the top three. All these products sell well both at home and abroad, thus winning Henan the reputations as "China's granary", "China's kitchen" and "China's dinner table".

I. China's "Granary"

In May, 2014, President Xi Jinping pointed out that Henan should hold on tight to its advantage of crop production by centering on the goal of building the "big granary" of China during his inspection tour in Henan. Now, 95 of the 106 counties in Henan are big grain-producing counties. In the context of structural adjustment, Henan implemented the strategy of developing high-standard cropland and agricultural technology to ensure the comprehensive production capacity of grain and became the national grain production core area. Since 2004, the crop production has increased for 12 years in a row, exceeding 90 billion, 100 billion, 110 billion and 120 billion *jin* (1 *jin* =0.5 kg) in succession. Therefore, the grain production of Henan has accounted for 1/10 of the country's total while its cropland only keeps to 1/16, of which, the wheat yield has reached 70 billion *jin*, accounting for 27% of the country's total.

中国第二；羊4 000多万只，居中国第四。2016年，河南省畜牧业产值2 611亿元，居中国第一位。河南真正成了中国人的"大粮仓"。

二、中国人的"大厨房"

2007年，"大粮仓"雏形基本建成后，河南以食品加工为突破口，重点扶持市场潜力大、附加值高的农副产品加工企业，拉开了河南由"大粮仓"向"大厨房"转变的序幕。自此，河南的馒头、饺子、汤圆等食品加工业迅速发展，河南很快实现了由"卖原粮"到"卖产品"、由"天下粮仓"到"国人厨房"的转变。

河南是中国第一粮食转化加工大省、第一肉制品大省、第一肉牛大省。河南速冻水饺产量占全国的85%，汤圆占75%，火腿肠占50%，每3包方便面有1包产自河南，每4个馒头有1个产自河南。双汇集团年销售

联合收割机在正阳县的高标准粮田里收割小麦
Combine harvesters are harvesting wheat in high-standard grain fields in Zhengyang County

Since 2014, agricultural supply-side structural reform has been implemented in Henan, focusing on the development of "high quality wheat, peanut, grassland and livestock, fruit and vegetable". As a result, Henan, as the "big granary", has an abundant supply of grains as well as meat, eggs and milk. Henan ranks the top for its livestock and poultry output. Among which, cattle raising ranks the first with a total of 14 million, pig raising and poultry raising the second with a total of 100 million and 1.6 billion, goat and sheep raising the fourth with a total of more than 40 million. In 2016, the output value of animal husbandry reached 261.1 billion *yuan*, which ranks the first in the whole country. Henan is truly worth the name of "China's Granary".

II. China's "Kitchen"

In 2007, when the "granary" was basically built, taking food processing as a breakthrough, Henan gave special support to agricultural and sideline products processing enterprises with great market potential and high added value. Therefore, the prologue of its transition from "granary" to "kitchen" was opened. Since then, the food processing industry in Henan, such as the production of mantou (steamed bread), jiaozi (dumpling), and tangyuan (sweet dumpling), has been flourishing, which indeed speeds up the transition of Henan from "grain production" to "food processing".

In terms of beef cattle and meat products, Henan is equally the most important producer nationwide. Statistics show the percentages of food processing of Henan in China, including fast-frozen jiaozi, 85%, tangyuan, 75%, ham sausage, 50%, instant noodle, 33%, mantou, 25%. There are three leading agricultural and sideline products processing enterprises in Henan. One is Shuanghui Group, the largest pork processor in China, whose annual sales income is 135 billion *yuan*. The other two are Sanquan Foods Co., Ltd and Synear Food Holdings Limited. As the pioneers of fast-frozen food in China, they are the major producers of fast-frozen food with jiaozi and tangyuan as their key products. In 2016, Sanquan frozen jiaozi occupied China's market by 48%, and as to the production of tangyuan, the two companies provided 50% of the country's total. As more and more Henan elements walk into the kitchen of Chinese households, Henan has developed from the "granary" into the "kitchen" of Chinese people.

收入1 350亿元，是全球规模最大、布局最广、产业链最完善、最具竞争力的猪肉加工企业。三全、思念是中国速冻食品的开拓者。2017年，中国生产速冻水饺127.2亿个，三全占了48%；中国生产汤圆131.3亿个，三全和思念加起来占到了50%。中国百姓厨房里的河南元素愈来愈多，河南已由中国人的"大粮仓"变为中国人的"大厨房"。

三、中国人的"大餐桌"

现在，河南已经开始谋划如何在"大粮仓"的基础上，实现"大厨房"的再次转变，延伸产业链条，生产可以直接入口的食品，搭起中国人的"大餐桌"。中国人的"大餐桌"可以概括为四种。

1. 居家餐桌

双汇、三全、思念等品牌餐桌食品久负盛名，家喻户晓。三全研发

双汇集团的生产车间
The Workshop of Shuanghui Group

III. China's "Dinner Table"

On the basis of the "granary", Henan has begun to plan how to further deepen the industrialization of the "kitchen" and produce ready-to-eat food, so as to set up the "dinner table" for Chinese people, which can be summed up as four categories:

1. Household "Dinner Table"

Shuanghui, Sanquan, Synear are well known enterprises for their processed food or instant food. A good case in point is Sanquan's self-heating food which is very convenient to eat. Other brands like Bingyu, Yuchu from Pubei Food Co., Ltd. in Xinxiang City are popular raw materials and semi-finished food products, selling well in China. Instant udon noodles from Yanjin Keming Noodles Co., Ltd. also enjoy equal popularity all over China. The quality of Dongyuan high-end fermented ham developed by Chuying Agro-Pastoral Group is comparable to that of Spanish high-end ham. Accordingly, Henan brand food products, with their high quality, delicacy and convenience, have made their way to the dinner tables in thousands of Chinese households, making people's life easier and more comfortable.

2. Pastoral "Dinner Table"

The table is set at the bamboo forest or by the brook. All the food ingredients come from the nearby fields, being zero pollution and organic from planting to processing. The annual reception of pastoral dinner table in Henan amounts to over 90 million. The pastoral dinner table reveals a vivid picture of beautiful countryside with its vitality.

3. Business "Dinner Table"

Sanquan Foods Co., Ltd has already developed its third generation of dinning table food which covers over 200 varieties, including dishes, set meals, rice balls, desserts and Western food, etc. A brand-new dinning model of "central kitchen+ APP+ terminal vending machine" has been created to meet the needs of white collar workers. At present, intelligent convenience stores have been set up equipped with 1,000 sets of O2O terminal vending machines, which are especially welcomed by young people, for they can order what they prefer with their cell phones.

的自加热食品，十分方便快捷；新乡市蒲北食品有限公司开发的冰宇、豫厨品牌菜品原料及半成品食材产品，畅销全中国；延津克明面业股份有限公司开发的即食乌冬面，方便美味，供不应求；雏鹰农牧集团开发的东元高端发酵火腿，品质可与西班牙的高端火腿媲美。河南产品摆上了千家万户的餐桌，让人们的生活变得更加轻松、惬意。

2. 田园餐桌

餐桌摆在竹林边、小溪旁，各种食材来自桌边的田地，从种植到加工，零污染，全有机。河南的田园餐桌每年接待客人9 000多万人次。一张张田园餐桌组成一幅美丽的乡村画卷。

3. 商务餐桌

河南三全食品公司的餐桌食品已发展到第三代，涵盖各种菜肴、套餐、饭团、甜品及西餐食品等200多个单品，采用"中央厨房+APP（应用程序）+终端售卖机"形式，创造了一种全新的餐饮模式，来满足办公室白领们的用餐需求。目前，在全国开设了智能便利店，投放了1 000多台O2O（线上到线下）终端售卖机，上班点手机预定，下班取菜就餐，快捷便利，深受年轻人欢迎。

4. 太空餐桌

河南永达食业集团连续多年为中国宇航员提供太空食品。永达公司生产的八珍烧鸡、奶香鸡米、蘑菇鸡块等航天食品，让航天员的餐桌变得琳琅满目。

河南农业从"大粮仓"到"大厨房"，再到"大餐桌"的发展实

4. Space "Dinner Table"

Henan Yongda Food Co., Ltd. is the major supplier of space food for Chinese astronauts. They produce different varieties of space food for astronauts to choose from, such as roast chicken, mushroom chicken nuggets and so on.

In the development of Henan agriculture from the building of "granary" to "kitchen" and "dinner table", three revolutions on agriculture, food and people's way of living have been generated. This miraculous transition makes Henan a strong agricultural province whose farmers are becoming well-off.

IV. The Rural Vitalization in Henan

The implementation of the strategy of rural vitalization is a major policy decision made by the 19th National Congress of the CPC. The overall requirements of rural vitalization was put forward, including thriving businesses, pleasant living environments, social etiquette and civility, effective governance and prosperity. In the new stage of reform and opening up, Henan's agriculture and its rural areas are undergoing historic changes. In terms of its agriculture, significant progress has been made in structural reform on the supply side of agriculture and grain production. New businesses in rural areas are developing in a thriving way and agricultural modernization is developing in a steady way. In today's rural areas of Henan, farmers enjoy a more beautiful living environment with increasingly improved public service facilities. In addition, more and more poor villages achieve poverty alleviation with the growth rate of the villagers' income higher than that of urban residents in successive years. Integration of urban and rural areas has become a historical trend. Henan is on its way of rural vitalization, where agriculture is becoming a promising business, farmer an appealing profession and rural areas more livable and beautiful places.

1. Agriculture Becoming a Promising Business

The autumn of 2017 saw a bumper harvest in Menglou Town, Dengzhou City. However, they used to have a meager income by keeping busy all the year around in the fields. In 2016, based on the land certification, Rural Land Development Co., Ltd. was set up in Dengzhou City to turn dry land into irrigated one through land consolidation project. 98% of the farmland is circulated via the company, which makes it possible that farmers can not only get their rent

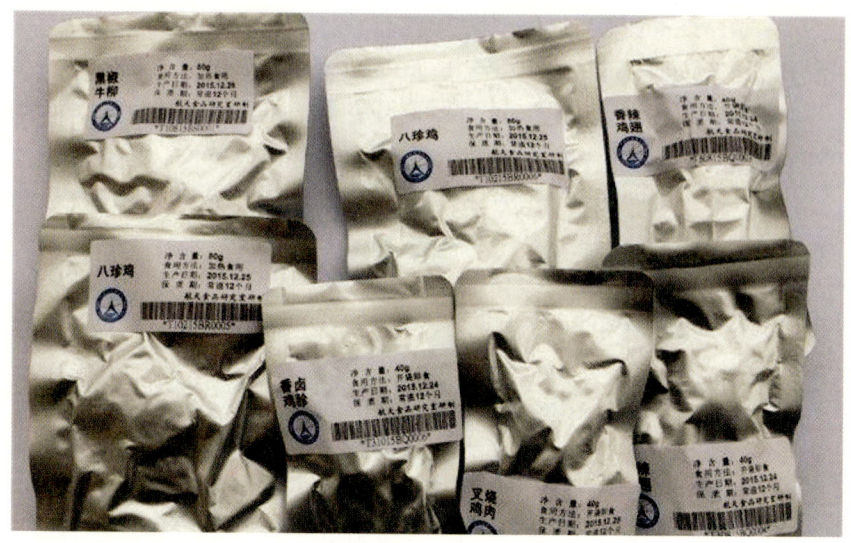

永达公司生产的航天食品
Space food for Chinese astronauts produced by Yongda Food Co., Ltd.

践,引发了农业革命、食品革命以及生活方式的革命,这是一个神奇的转变,让河南从农业大省变成了农业强省,让农民的腰包真正鼓了起来。

四、河南乡村在振兴

　　实施乡村振兴战略,是党的十九大作出的重大决策部署,提出了"产业兴旺、生态宜居、乡风文明、治理有效、生活富裕"的乡村振兴总体要求。改革开放进入了新时代,河南农业、农村正在发生着历史性变革。农业供给侧结构性改革取得新进展,粮食生产能力跨上新台阶,农村新产业、新业态蓬勃发展,农业现代化稳步推进。如今的河南农村,人居环境变得越来越美,公共服务设施日益完善,越来越多的贫困户和贫困村摘掉了穷帽子,农民收入增速连年高于城镇居民,城乡融合发展成为历史发展趋势。让农业成为有奔头的产业,让农民成为有吸引力的职业,让农村成为安居乐业的美丽家园,河南乡村正在振兴。

without doing farm work, but also earn a salary in the company. Moreover, the young and middle-aged migrant workers do not have to be back to do farm work during the busy seasons. Land consolidation has made scale management possible, resulting in the signing on agreement of circulation of rural land contracted management right between new type of agribusinesses and Dengzhou Rural Land Development Co., Ltd.

Farmers in Menglou Town and these agribusinesses that have contracted land here benefit from the system for separating rural land ownership rights, contract rights, and management rights for contracted rural land. The exploration of the system makes farming a brilliant prospect.

2. Farmer Becoming an Appealing Profession

Here is a successful example of eight post-90s college students who work as professional farmers in Tianhua Agricultural Cooperative, Weiji Town, Shangshui County. Most of them major in agricultural machinery and agriculture with experience of new type of farmers training. Seven of them have learned UAV control technology and the operation and maintenance of large tractors. Their annual income reaches fifty to sixty thousand *yuan*. They believe that modern agriculture needs educated young people who have a good knowledge of agriculture, love rural areas, and care about rural people, and they can surely act as bellwethers.

With the emergence of new types of agribusinesses, such as family farms, farmer cooperatives, leading enterprises in agricultural industrialization and so on, there are more and more various training opportunities for farmers and therefore traditional farmers are replaced by new professional farmers like those post-90s college students mentioned above. This is especially typical among the rural young who are equipped with knowledge, techniques and ability to learn. Farmer, like worker, company employee and teacher, has become an appealing profession.

3. Rural Areas Becoming More Livable and Beautiful

Great changes have taken place in Xixinzhuang village, Puyang City, where villagers live in rows of buildings surrounded by fruit trees and vegetables. Li Yuxing, 55 years old, is a good case in point. He works in the logistics service department of a local hospital with a monthly salary of about three to four thousand *yuan*, while his wife can earn two thousand *yuan* doing some odd jobs each month. Their courtyard is full of fruit trees, such as pomegranate, walnut,

1. 让农业成为有奔头的产业

2017年的秋天，对邓州市孟楼镇的农民来说，是一个丰收的秋天。过去，他们守着零零散散的岗坡地"望天收"，一年忙到头，收入微薄。2016年，在土地确权颁证的基础上，邓州市成立了农村土地开发有限公司，借助土地整理项目，把旱地变成了水浇良田。98%的耕地通过公司集中流转，农民不用耕种，就拿到了租金，还能去公司打工挣一份工资，在外务工的青壮年也不用在农忙时请假回家。土地经过规整，有了规模经营的可能，吸引了几十家新型农业经营主体与邓州市农村土地开发有限公司签订经营权流转协议。

孟楼镇的农民和这些来此"包地"的新型农业经营主体正是河南土地所有权、承包权、经营权"三权分置"探索的受益者。"三权分置"探索让农业成了更多人眼里有"钱途"的事业。

2. 让农民成为有吸引力的职业

在商水县魏集镇天华种植专业合作社里，有8个种粮食的90后大学生。他们大多是学农机、农业的，参加过新型农民培训，其中7个人还去学习过无人机操控技术及大型拖拉机的操作与维修。他们每人每月有2 000元底薪，加上作业提成，一年净收入五六万元。他们说："未来农民会成为一个有吸引力的职业。现在到了有知识、有文化的年轻人种地的时候了，我们懂农业、爱农村、爱农民，有信心当好领头羊。"

可喜的是，随着家庭农场、农民合作社、农业产业化龙头企业、专业大户等新型农业经营主体的大批涌现，各种学习、培训的机会增多，传统意义上的农民越来越少，和天华种植专业合作社的那些90后大学生一样的新型职业农民越来越多。这种情况在乡村年轻人中尤为突出，他们有文化、有技术、会学习，和父辈已完全不同，农民已逐渐成为有吸

hawthorn, peach etc., so comfortable to live that they refuse to move to the city where their child lives. Nowadays, the clean and quiet village is well equipped with various facilities including schools, hospitals, stores, hotels, restaurants and so on.

Another example is a small mountain village named Liuzhuang located in Mianchi County, Sanmenxia City. In the past, this village was surrounded by barren mountains and wasteland and was known for its poverty. However, those days are gone. With the persistent efforts in changing its backwardness, such as building dams, greening barren mountains and so on, this poor village has now turned into a "star village" famous for its beautiful scenery. The agricultural tourism here has brought villagers an income increase from 5,000 *yuan* to 17,000 *yuan* per person each year. All the villagers including poverty-stricken ones live in new buildings.

These dramatic changes taking place in many villages of Henan indicate that we are approaching the goal of making our rural areas more livable and beautiful.

V. The Construction of a Beautiful Henan

President Xi Jinping pointed out that a beautiful China should be built on the basis of the construction of the beautiful villages, and the truth that lucid waters and lush mountains are invaluable assets has been confirmed by the development of eco-tourism economy and construction of beautiful villages. He has also put forward that the development-oriented poverty reduction should be combined with the construction of beautiful villages.

Henan responded actively to the Construction of Beautiful Villages initiative and has achieved remarkable achievements. More and more picturesque villages are built either on economic development or through poverty alleviation. In accordance with the strategic requirements of agriculture and rural area development, people stick to the practice of preserving the original ecological environments by adding cultural connotation to them in the process of building these beautiful villages, thus meeting the farmers' increasing needs for a better life.

The three mainstay industries in building beautiful villages are economic development, ecological construction and historical culture preservation. In recent three years, the provincial government of Henan has invested a great amount of money in developing rural industries and improving rural ecological

河南省商水县天华种植专业合作社的植物保护无人直升机升空作业
The pilotless helicopter of Tianhua Agricultural Cooperative in Shangshui County is performing plant protection

引力的职业。

3. 让农村成为安居乐业的美丽家园

河南濮阳西辛庄村远近闻名,村民住的房子大都是一排排一样高的小楼,院子里和院墙外种满果树和蔬菜。李玉星的小院里种了石榴、核桃、山楂、桃子等果树,收拾得干干净净。他现在在西辛庄民生医院后勤部门工作,每个月能拿三四千元,他的妻子干些杂活一个月也能挣两千元钱。他说,他的孩子给他在城里买了房,他不去。现在,村里学校、医院、超市、宾馆、饭店、文化广场,啥都有,到处干干净净、清清静静的,比城里还好。

柳庄村是三门峡渑池县的一个小山村。"眼前乱石滩,四周是荒

environment in order to promote the common growth of material wealth as well as the ecological one, and the environmental quality as well as the living quality of farmers. Up to now, we have built 900 beautiful villages, 13 state-level livable towns, 39 state-level livable villages. A picture of ecological, beautiful and livable villages with flat roads, clean yards and green surroundings can be seen everywhere in Henan.

1. Making Use of Garbage to Generate Electricity

Tielu village of Zhangpan Town, in which garbage was found here and there, is very clean now. Where has the garbage gone? It turns out that Jian'an District, Xuchang City, has invested over 40 million *yuan* in building beautiful villages. It entrusts two enterprises to clear garbage of the village and send it to the power plant. By government purchasing service and planning garbage treatment as a whole, Henan carries out the model of "household placing, village collecting, town transferring, county disposing" to deal with the garbage in the countryside in a stable and smooth way.

2. Villages Becoming Brighter and More Beautiful

"Our village has garbage cans and cleaners. Clean water is drawn into ditches which are lined with landscape trees. The whole village is just like a large garden." Remarked Hao Daocheng, a 78-year-old villager of Haolou village, Dancheng County. Such beautiful villages like Haolou are frequently seen in Central China. Since 2016, Henan Province has accumulatively invested 35 billion *yuan* in building 38 thousand kilometers of roads, which greatly improved the transporting conditions of the villagers. In Henan, 85% of the administrative villages can enjoy tap water, and 65% of the households can cook with coal gas, natural gas and liquefied petroleum gas. The power lines in 6,989 central villages have been transformed and upgraded, so 9,200 villages can use dynamic electricity. The important areas in 80% of the administrative villages are illuminated at night.

3. Developing Colorful Agritainment Sightseeing Gardens

The activity of building green homeland has been launched all over Henan, with the green coverage ratio in the countryside reaching 24.5%. Xuchang carried out the project of "turning one residence into four different gardens", which refers to turning a wasted residence into sightseeing garden, flower garden, tree garden, and vegetable garden or orchard. Xuchang renovated 16,000 *mu* deserted residence and built over 3,000 sightseeing gardens. This brought beauty and

山；一条羊肠道，通往山外边；每逢雨季来，心惊又胆战；姑娘往外嫁，小伙娶妻难，十里八乡成笑谈。"这段顺口溜是昔日村子的写照。如今，在党支部的带领下，当地村民修大坝，治荒山，建新村，这个贫穷的山村已华丽转身，成了远近闻名的风光秀美的明星村，成了很多城里人游玩的好去处。村民人均年收入由过去的不足5 000元上升到1.7万元，村里所有的贫困户都住上了统一规划设计的"小洋楼"。

除了西辛庄、柳庄，还有很多乡村变得让人羡慕，让农村成为安居乐业的美丽家园，这个目标在一点点变成现实。

五、美丽河南在行动

习近平总书记指出，"美丽中国要靠美丽乡村打基础，发展生态旅游经济、建设美丽乡村印证了绿水青山就是金山银山的道理"，"要把扶贫开发与富在农家、学在农家、乐在农家、美在农家的美丽乡村建设结合起来"。

河南各地积极行动，美丽乡村建设取得了瞩目成就，涌现出一批秀美如画的乡村。这些美丽乡村有的是在经济发展的基础上建设的，有的是通过脱贫攻坚改变了村里的面貌。这些美丽乡村的建设大都是坚持不挖山、不填塘、不砍树、不大拆大建，本着留住乡愁，注入文化内涵，按照农业农村发展的战略要求，与时俱进，进行"升级"，从而更符合广大农民群众日益增长的美好生活需求。

经济发展、生态建设、历史文化保护是美丽乡村建设的三大支柱产业。近年来，河南集中财力，发展农村产业，提升农村生态环境，推动社会物质财富与生态财富共同增长，社会环境质量与农民生活质量同步提高。河南全省已建成900个美丽村庄、13个国家级美丽宜居小镇、39个国家级美丽宜居村庄。行走在中原大地，村庄道路平坦，庭院干净，绿树环合，越来越多的乡村变得更加生态化、美丽、宜居。

wealth to farmers. Xinyang rebuilt the rural culture to promote the economic development. The counties with better ecological environment, such as Shihe District, Xinxian County, Shangcheng County, have realized all-for-one tourism. Half of 198 towns have become tourist towns or leisure agriculture towns. The total income of rural tourism was about 270 million *yuan* in 2017.

4. Attaching Importance to Both External and Internal Beauty

In building beautiful villages, external beauty is just one side, while internal beauty is more important, that is, both ecological and cultural constructions should keep abreast.

For instance, in Yuxian village, Yucheng County, villagers learn from the folklores and stories which are handed down from generation to generation telling about how to get along with neighbors and friends to develop harmonious relationship between neighbors and the sense of righteousness in making friends. Another example is Haotang village in Xinyang. Its beauty is not only presented by 100 *mu* of lotus ponds covered by green leaves and the old trees dotting in the village, but more importantly, it lies in the retaining of its original ecology, its development full of inspiring stories, and its features of tranquility, primitive simplicity and leisure. And Liuzhuang village in Xinxiang is featured by its collective economy. The sacrificing spirit of selflessness and the idea of achieving common prosperity for all have passed down from the senior generation of Shi Laihe (the former Party secretary of Liuzhuang village, a nationally renowned model worker).

The building of "a Beautiful Henan" needs more beautiful villages. Since 2013, the provincial administration has been undertaking the construction of "Beautiful Villages", focusing on the construction of livable towns, central villages and characteristic villages. 430 pilot constructions of beautiful villages have been determined and carried out by adjusting measures to local conditions, setting up projects through scientific competition, and breaking through constructing difficulties. This certainly helps to promote the equalization of public services, to integrate the urban and rural areas and to improve the living environment of farmers.

Ⅵ. Win the Critical Battle Against Poverty

In March 2014, while the spring wind was blowing with mighty power, the General Secretary of Central Committee of the CPC Xi Jinping made an

1. 村里垃圾送去发电

许昌市建安区张潘镇铁炉村，原来村里的垃圾这儿一堆那儿一堆，现在却不见了踪影。村里的垃圾到哪儿去了？原来，近年来，建安区投入4 000多万元推进美丽乡村建设，委托两家企业负责垃圾清运处理，村里每天的垃圾都被送到了发电厂。河南通过政府购买服务，统筹城乡垃圾处理工作，实行"户投放、村收集、乡转运、县处理"的模式，让农村垃圾有了稳定而畅通的处理渠道。

2. 村庄变得更亮更美

"我们村有了垃圾桶，还有保洁员。河沟引来了清水，两边栽上了绿化树，村庄就像大公园。"郸城县胡集乡郝楼村78岁的郝道成说。像郝楼这样的村庄，在中原大地越来越多。2016年以来，河南省累计完成投资350亿元，建成农村公路3.8万公里，村民出行条件明显改善；河南省85%的行政村使用自来水，65%的农户使用煤气、天然气、液化石油气做饭；累计完成6 989个中心村电网改造升级，9 200个自然村通上动力电；80%的行政村公共场所等重点部位夜间有了照明。

3. 多彩田园力促振兴

河南各地大力开展绿色家园创建活动，乡村绿化覆盖率达24.5%。许昌市大力推进"一宅变四园"行动，将荒芜宅院整治成游园、花园、树园、菜（果）园，整治荒芜宅基地1.6万亩，打造游园3 000多个。不仅要让农村更美，还要让农民更富。信阳市重塑乡村文化内涵，带动村庄经济发展。浉河区及新县、商城县等生态较好的县区基本实现了全域旅游。全市198个乡镇中近半数成为旅游小镇、休闲农业小镇，2017

inspection tour in Lankao County, Henan Province, directing the Party's second batch of mass line educational campaign and leaving ardent entrustment to the Party members. As Xi urged, in the critical battle against poverty, the county should enrich its people while enhancing its strength, combine the reform with development, and connect urban and rural areas. Besides, the Party members and cadres should carry forward the spirit of Jiao Yulu — the model of all cadres, and seize the opportunity to lift Lankao out of poverty.

Over the past six years, CPC Henan Provincial Committee and Henan Provincial People's Government have been battling against poverty throughout the overall economic and social development by adhering to the basic strategy of targeted poverty alleviation. With the concerted efforts of government officials and people, more progress has been made in the poverty elimination and the pursuit of a decisive victory in building a moderately prosperous society in all respects.

1. Industry Leading Being the Key to Poverty Alleviation

In Xuchang village of Guyang Town in Lankao County, the paulownia woods originally as windbreaks help 21 local households, totaling 102 villagers, eradicate poverty. By producing folk musical instruments with paulownia trees, the per capita annual income of the village surpasses 30,000 yuan. In Duzhai village, villagers led by a poverty-alleviation team plant melons in the old course of the Yellow River, making 43 households get rid of poverty. In Zhangzhuang village of Dongbatou Town, cadres and villagers work together to build a beautiful countryside, attracting over 100,000 tourists every year.

From 2014 to 2017, Lankao has formed a three-dimensional industrial layout which consists of furniture, breeding and new energy. The integrated development of primary, secondary and tertiary industries has brought the county a growth in its comprehensive strength from the lower middle level to the top tier among counties in Henan Province. In March 2017, Lankao, together with Jinggangshan City in Jiangxi Province, took the lead in eliminating poverty across the country, and was the first impoverished county to shake off poverty in Henan Province. Since then, other impoverished counties in Henan, with targeted strategy, have been following Lankao's example, to develop their specialty industries in light of the local resources and conditions.

Mountainous counties began to live on their ecological conditions. For

年，乡村旅游景点营业收入约为2.7亿元。

4. 看"颜值"，更要看"气质"

建设美丽乡村，外表美是一方面，更重要的是内涵美，生态建设和文化建设齐头并进。

虞城县田庙乡寓贤村，古称石门山寨，即孔子《论语》中"子路宿于石门"的地方，利用"编笆接枣，锯树留邻"的传说和"空壶留故友，削发待宾朋"的佳话，依托"待邻寺"和"待宾寺"的遗址遗迹，重点培养一种和谐的邻里关系，以及重义恋情的朋友相处之道。信阳郝堂村之美，不仅在于村头碧叶连天的百亩荷塘和散布村落的百年古树，更在于其原生态住房保留了传统之美、乡村之魂，在于郝堂村声名鹊起的"励志"历程，在于其静谧、古朴、闲适的气质；新乡县刘庄之美，不仅在于集体经济风生水起，更在于史来贺等老一辈干部传承下来的公而忘私的奉献精神，在于其共享发展、共同富裕的为民理念。

"美丽河南"需要更多美丽乡村。2013年以来，河南启动美丽乡村建设试点工作，重点培育建设美丽宜居小镇、中心村及特色村。因地制宜谋划，科学竞争立项，突破建设难点，确定430个试点项目，项目的实施对推进农村基本公共服务均等化、改善农村人居环境、提升农民生活品质、促进城乡一体化等起到了有力的推动作用，铺开了"美丽乡村"新画卷。

六、打赢脱贫攻坚战

2014年3月，春风浩荡。习近平总书记来到河南兰考，调研指导第二批党的群众路线教育实践活动，留下殷殷嘱托。他要求兰考在脱贫攻坚的战役中，把强县和富民统一起来，把改革和发展结合起来，把城镇

example, Xichuan County, at the water-head area of the central line of South-to-North Water Project, sticks to the idea of combining eco-environmental protection with poverty alleviation by developing economic crop planting. It has planted soft seeds pomegranates of 32,000 *mu*, thin-shelled walnuts of over 0.1 million *mu* and Chinese medical herbs of over 40,000 *mu*, such as Jinyinhua (honeysuckle), Xinyi (magnolia), Duzhong (eucommia), and Aicao (artemisia). Thereupon, not only the eco-environment is well protected, but the livelihood of 0.1 million farmers in the area is improved.

Plain counties have cultivated their "golden beans" — peanuts. With underdeveloped industry and low fiscal revenue, some of the plain counties seek ways to get rid of poverty. For example, Zhengyang County has expanded and strengthened peanuts industry while stabilizing the sown area of grain and ensuring national food security. At present, the county grows 1.7 million *mu* high quality peanuts every year, lifting tens of thousands of villagers out of poverty by changing the "small peanuts" into the "golden beans".

Beach area counties have set up their "new workshops". Those impoverished counties located in the beach areas of the Yellow River are making endeavors to eradicate poverty based on the local condition. For example, Taiqian County made bold explorations by building, renovating or expanding 124 employment bases for targeted poverty alleviation in 2016, which offered 8,090 jobs, and 3,562 of them were taken by the impoverished people. Nowadays, such win-win workshops are booming across the province.

Thanks to the promotion by poverty alleviation industries, the economy of the impoverished counties in Henan Province has seen rapid growth in the past six years. The per capita disposable income of rural residents has been steadily increasing, with a growth rate higher than the province's average. Of all the poverty alleviation industries, the top ten advanced and characteristic agricultural industries, such as quality wheat, peanuts, forage livestock, forest fruit and Chinese medicinal materials, have mobilized and benefited 1.93 million impoverished people. 3,811 poverty alleviation workshops have been set up, benefiting 51,000 poor people. Tourism has emerged, promoting about 60,000 people's poverty elimination. E-commerce industry has been gathering momentum, helping 59,300 poor villagers with employment and self-employment.

和乡村贯通起来。党员干部要大力弘扬焦裕禄精神，抓住机遇，彻底改变兰考的贫困面貌。

6年来，河南省委、省政府持续以脱贫攻坚贯穿经济社会发展全局，坚持精准扶贫精准脱贫基本方略，带领广大干部群众勠力同心、众志成城，决战脱贫攻坚、决胜全面小康，书写出了更加绚丽的篇章。

1. 脱贫攻坚，产业引领是关键

在兰考县堌阳镇徐场村，曾经遮挡风沙的泡桐林成了制作民族乐器的"绿色银行"，助力21户102人脱贫，全村人均年收入超过3万元；在葡萄架乡杜寨村，扶贫工作队带领群众在黄河故道种起蜜瓜，带动村里43户贫困户脱贫；在东坝头镇张庄村，干部群众齐心协力打造美丽乡村，"梦里张庄"名闻遐迩，每年接待游客超10万人次……

2014年至2017年，兰考县形成了家居、养殖、新能源立体式发展的产业格局，实现一二三产业融合发展，综合实力从全省县域中下游跃升到第一方阵。2017年3月，兰考县与革命圣地江西省井冈山市一起，在全国率先脱贫，打响了河南省贫困县摘帽"第一枪"。以兰考为标杆，以精准为方略，全省其他贫困县立足资源禀赋，因地制宜发展特色产业。

山区县吃上"生态饭"。南水北调中线渠首所在地淅川县结合实际，坚持"绿色扶贫"思路，发展软籽石榴种植面积3.2万亩，种植薄壳核桃等10万余亩，发展金银花、辛夷、杜仲、艾草等中药材种植面积4万余亩，10万渠首农民端上"绿饭碗"。

平原县培育"金豆豆"。工业弱、财政穷，怎么办？正阳县在稳定粮食面积和保障国家粮食安全的前提下，做大做强花生产业。目前，该县每年种植优质花生170万亩，带动全县上万名贫困群众脱贫，把"小花生"变成了"金豆豆"。

2. The Integration of Reform and Development Being the Driving Force to Poverty Alleviation

To achieve poverty alleviation, reform and development should be closely integrated. Reform is a magic "weapon" in promoting development, while development is the "key" to solutions. Over the past six years, reform and development ran through the whole process of poverty alleviation in Henan Province, providing inexhaustible impetus for this great cause.

In December 2016, approved by the State Council, Lankao County became the first inclusive finance reform pilot zone in China. The inclusive finance reform, which changed the traditional "credit + credit and loan" into "credit and loan + credit", broke the "barrier" between farmers and banks and brought financial support for the development of enterprises, and hence becoming the "invisible booster" for Lankao's poverty alleviation.

"The inclusive finance is like the timely rain." said Yuan Xinzhong, a villager of Lixi village, Guying Town. In 2017, he set up two vegetable greenhouses by loan, becoming the first person in the village to lift himself out of poverty. By July 2018, Lankao County had issued inclusive financial credit cards to more than 160,000 households, basically achieving the goal of "inclusive credit for all households".

Under the guidance of solving capital problems and with the support of establishing financial service system, credit evaluation system, industrial support system and risk prevention and control system, Lushi County, the poorest county in Henan Province, found a new model of financial poverty alleviation which is well known in the whole country.

In practice, Lushi County not only provided "one-to-one" service for the people who are able to work, but also satisfied the large financing needs of leading enterprises that help to lift the villagers out of poverty through the mutual aid mode among "government, enterprise and bank", achieving exponential increase of the poverty reduction effect. Henan Lushi Rural Commercial Bank Co., Ltd. alone has provided more than 1 billion RMB of poverty-relief loans to 7,884 poverty-stricken households. Henan Xinnian Group, a leading anti-poverty enterprise, has invested in the construction of three ecological pig farms, more than 300 vegetable greenhouses and 13 mushroom bases in more than 10 towns and villages, providing jobs for more than 10,000 impoverished people.

滩区县建起"新车间"。扶贫安得"双全法",既能挣钱又顾家?2016年,地处黄河滩区的台前县大胆探索,新建和改扩建精准扶贫就业基地124个,吸纳就业8 090人,其中贫困群众3 562人。如今,让多方共赢的扶贫车间已在全省遍地开花。

6年来,在扶贫产业的有力推动下,河南省贫困县县域经济得到长足发展,农村居民人均可支配收入"节节高",增幅高于全省平均水平。其中,优质小麦、花生、草畜、林果、中药材等十大优势特色农业,覆盖带动贫困人口193万人;规范建成扶贫车间3 811个,受益贫困人口5.1万人;旅游产业异军突起,带动贫困人口约6万人;电商产业持续壮大,带动贫困人口就业创业5.93万人。

2. 脱贫攻坚,改革和发展紧密结合

改革是推动发展的"法宝",发展是破解难题的"钥匙"。6年来,改革和发展贯穿河南省脱贫攻坚全部进程,为这一伟大事业提供不竭动力。

2016年12月,经国务院批准,我国首个普惠金融改革试验区花落兰考。普惠金融改革变传统的"信用+信贷"为"信贷+信用",打破了农民和银行间的"玻璃墙",引来了企业发展的"源头活水",成为兰考脱贫的"隐形功臣"。

"普惠金融给俺的感觉就像是'贴心小棉袄'。"谷营镇栗西村村民袁新中说。2017年,他贷款盖起两座蔬菜大棚,在全村第一个脱贫摘帽。截至2018年7月,兰考县已为16万余户农户发放普惠金融授信证,基本实现"普惠授信户户全覆盖"的目标。

河南省贫困程度最深的卢氏县,以破解资金难题为导向,以建好金融服务体系、信用评价体系、产业支撑体系和风险防控体系为支撑,探索出叫响全国的金融扶贫新模式。

In recent years, Henan Province, by improving the system for separating the ownership rights, contract rights, and management rights for contracted rural land, has further pressed ahead with reform of the rural collective property rights system, promoted the two-way interchange and equal exchange of talents, land, capital and other factors between urban and rural areas, so as to promote the effective linking up of poverty relief and the rural revitalization.

Depending on their beautiful natural scenery — the green mountains and blue waters, villagers organized by Share-holding Economic Co-operative in Pudian village, Shawo Town, Xinxian County held the first Peach Flower Festival in March 2019, which attracted more than 10,000 tourists and boomed 53 agritainments in the village. Xiaoguanzhuang village, Zhonghe Town, Huojia County used to be a very poor village. However, after the reform of the collective property right system, the village cooperated with a local enterprise to build more than 160 edible fungus greenhouses, which allowed thousands of people around to increase their incomes steadily.

With the party branch of the village steering and the village committee in charge of affairs, shareholding economic co-operative focusing on development, the reform of rural collective property rights system has turned resources into assets, capitals into shares, farmers into stockholders, which not only granted farmers capital stock certificate for the first time, but also identified the rural collective economic organizations as legal persons, and accordingly moving towards an extensive market.

By the end of 2019, 60% of administrative villages in Henan Province had basically completed the reform of the rural collective property rights system, according to an official from the Department of Agriculture and Rural Affairs of Henan Province. By the end of October 2020, all villages will have completed the reform so that the rural collective economy will grow from scratch, farmers' income from property will constantly increase and the path of shaking off poverty and getting rich will become more reliable.

3. The Coordinated Development of Urban and Rural Areas

To achieve poverty alleviation, the development of urban area and rural area should be coordinated. In 2017, Li Maitun, a villager from Donggangtou village, Yifeng Township, Lankao County, was planning to return home and start his own business, but he had doubts about his plan: Is it feasible to open a clothing store

在具体实践中，卢氏县既为有劳动能力的群众提供"一对一"服务，还通过"政企银"互助模式等，满足带贫龙头企业大额融资需求，减贫成效呈几何级增长。仅卢氏农商行一家，目前已累计投放扶贫贷款逾10亿元，为7 884户贫困户"雪中送炭"；扶贫龙头企业信念集团投资建设3个生态养猪场、300多座蔬菜大棚和13个香菇基地，覆盖十多个乡镇，带动1万余名贫困群众。

近年来，河南省还以完善农村承包土地"三权分置"改革为开端，深入推进农村集体产权制度改革，促使人才、土地、资本等要素在城乡间双向流动和平等交换，推动广袤乡村摆脱贫困，与乡村振兴有效衔接。

依托青山绿水，在村股份经济合作社组织下，新县沙窝镇朴店村2019年3月首次举办了桃花节，开幕当天就吸引游客1万多人，村里的53家农家乐生意火爆。获嘉县中和镇小官庄村原是当地有名的贫困村，在集体产权制度改革后，与当地一家企业合作，"无中生有"发展160多个食用菌大棚，带动周边上千名群众实现稳定增收。

资源变资产、资金变股金、农民变股东，党支部"把方向"，村委会"管事务"，股份经济合作社"抓发展"——农村集体产权制度改革不但让农民第一次有了股权证，也让农村集体经济组织有了"身份证"，成为真正的法人，迈向更加广阔的市场。

河南省农业农村厅相关负责人介绍，截至2019年底，全省60%的行政村基本完成农村集体产权制度改革；2020年10月底前，所有村要完成改革，让农村集体经济从无到有、从小变大，让农民群众财产性收入不断增加，脱贫致富之路更加坚实。

3. 脱贫攻坚，城镇和乡村交相辉映

2017年，兰考县仪封乡东岗头村村民李麦囤打算返乡创业，却又心

in the village? The cadre staying at his village persuaded him with the following words, "Now, with the development of urban-rural integration in the county, new communities have been built around our village, influencing the surrounding population of more than 10,000 people, so there should be a great market potential here."

The beautiful and livable countryside surprises the migrant villagers. Ever since the battle against poverty started, stories of people lifting themselves out of poverty have been going on all over Henan Province. For example, Liangshuiquan village of Lingshan Sub-District Community, about 8 kilometers away from Qixian County, used to be a poor mountainous village. After the poverty alleviation relocation in 2017, it was built into a high-end homestay wonderland. Villagers accordingly became workers in the scenic spot. Last year, the average income growth of every household in the village reached 23,500 *yuan*.

In recent years, Henan has strengthened planning guidance, investment guarantee and demand orientation, which gradually improves the level of infrastructure and public services in poverty-stricken areas, and makes weak links nearly level with the rest of the province. On the whole, the level of infrastructure construction in rural areas has achieved a historic leap, with prosperous towns and the beautiful villages enhancing each other.

Poverty alleviation by transportation projects has enabled each village to be linked by rural highways. A total of 7,980 kilometers of rural highways has been rebuilt in poverty-stricken areas, and the rate of cement pavement in administrative villages and the rate of public transportation in qualified administrative villages reached 100%. Of the 15 highway projects, 14 run through old revolutionary base areas, poverty-stricken areas or remote mountainous areas.

Poverty alleviation through water conservancy projects has quenched the thirst of villagers. A total of 1.761 billion *yuan* has been invested in the consolidation and upgrading of safe drinking water in rural areas, benefiting 2,443 administrative villages, including 933 poverty-stricken villages and 394,700 poverty stricken villagers, and realizing the full coverage of the documented status quo of drinking water security for poverty-stricken population in the province.

Achieving the formidable combination of power grid and internet. The transformation of power grids in poverty-stricken counties and villages has been completed ahead of schedule, which provides power supply to rural households,

存疑虑：在乡下开服装店，行不行？驻村干部一席话宽了他的心：如今县里城乡一体化大发展，咱村边都建了新社区，辐射周边1万多人口，市场潜力肯定大。

县城流光溢彩，乡村美丽宜居，让游子惊喜，令外人惊叹，脱贫攻坚战打响以来，这样的故事在河南各地不断"上演"。距淇县县城约8公里的灵山街道凉水泉村，原是个贫困的深石山村。2017年易地扶贫搬迁后，这里被打造成"灵泉妙境"高端民宿区，全村群众就地变成景区工人，去年，该村户均增收达2.35万元。

近年来，河南强化规划引领、投入保障和需求导向，使贫困地区的基础设施和公共服务水平逐步提升，各项短板明显补齐，农村基础设施建设水平整体上实现了历史性跃升，繁华城镇和美丽乡村交相辉映。

交通扶贫送"路"到村。新改建贫困地区农村公路7 980公里，行政村通硬化路率、具备条件的行政村通客车率均达100%。高速公路"双千工程"15个项目中，有14个经过革命老区、贫困地区或者偏远山区。

水利扶贫"解渴"入户。投入农村安全饮水巩固提升项目资金17.61亿元，受益行政村2 443个，其中贫困村933个，受益贫困人口39.47万人，实现全省建档立卡贫困人口饮水安全动态现状全覆盖。

电网、网络"双剑合璧"。提前完成贫困县、贫困村电网改造，全省农村户户通电、村村通动力电，全面实现20户以上自然村4G网络和光纤接入全覆盖。

环境整治"内外"翻新。以"千村示范、万村整治"工程为抓手，抓好农村垃圾治理、厕所革命、村容村貌提升，全省90%以上贫困村环境得到有效治理。

着眼于全面提升农村基本公共服务和社会保障水平，河南省同步开展健康扶贫、教育扶贫、易地扶贫搬迁、危房改造等多项扶贫开发重大行动，为农村地区发展添足后劲。

"目前，我省所有贫困县都已实现脱贫，651.1万名群众甩掉贫困

dynamic electricity to every village, and 4G network and optical fiber access to villages of more than 20 households.

Environment renovation in villages. Started from Green Rural Revival Program, rural garbage treatment, toilet revolution, and improvement of the appearance of villages have been completed, which has effectively improved the environment of more than 90% of poverty-stricken villages in the province.

With a view to comprehensively improving the level of basic public services and social security in rural areas, Henan Province has launched a number of major poverty alleviation and development initiatives, including poverty alleviation by health, poverty alleviation by education, poverty alleviation by relocation, and renovation of dilapidated houses, which have gathered more momentum for the sustainable development in rural areas.

"At present, all the counties in Henan Province have been removed from the poverty list according to the State Standard and 6,511,000 people have shaken off poverty. We have full confidence in the historic eradication of absolute poverty and the march toward a moderately prosperous society in all respects, but we cannot let up yet." said the person in charge of Henan Provincial Office of Poverty Alleviation and Development. We are facing the tough task of lifting the remaining 350,000 poverty-stricken population and 52 villages out of poverty in 2020 in Henan Province. And we are poised to win the battle against poverty.

Ⅶ. Going to the World of Henan Agriculture

Since 2016, CPC Henan Provincial Committee and Henan Provincial People's Government have been upholding the guiding principles of the 18th National Congress of the CPC and the 19th National Congress of the CPC. The construction of inland open highlands has been focused, agricultural transformation and upgrading propelled and the rural revitalization strategy implemented. Also, the rich agricultural resources and advantages of Henan have been given full play so as to get integrated into the construction of the Belt and Road, advance agricultural exchange and cooperation with other countries, and the agricultural supply-side structural reform. As a result, Henan agriculture is going to the world in a good momentum of steady growth.

帽。历史性地消灭绝对贫困，昂首迈向全面小康社会，我们信心十足，但还不能松懈。"河南省扶贫办相关负责人表示，2020年我省要完成35万贫困人口、52个贫困村脱贫摘帽的任务，不获全胜决不收兵。

七、河南农业走向世界

2016年以来，河南省委、省政府坚持以党的十八大精神和十九大最新精神为指引，紧紧围绕"打造内陆开放高地"、推进农业转型升级和落实乡村振兴战略总体部署，积极发挥河南农业资源丰富的优势，深度融入"一带一路"建设，统筹推进农业对外合作交流，积极助力农业供给侧结构性改革，河南农业走向世界呈现出持续向好、稳定有序的良性发展态势。

1. 河南农业走出去

截至目前，河南省在境外从事农业种植、养殖及深加工的企业有72家，分布于世界42个国家和地区，境外经营（租赁）土地面积超过450万亩。经营业务主要为三大类：玉米、小麦、棉花等粮食作物和经济作物种植，畜牧、养殖及肉类屠宰加工，食用菌、调味品等农副食品加工。合作国家除塔吉克斯坦、吉尔吉斯斯坦、乌兹别克斯坦、乌克兰、白俄罗斯、柬埔寨、巴基斯坦等"一带一路"沿线国家外，还延伸到美国、日本、澳大利亚等发达国家，以及尼日利亚、巴西等发展中国家。河南省黄泛区实业集团在塔吉克斯坦建设的中塔农业科技示范区受到了塔吉克斯坦总统的多次肯定。河南贵友实业集团在吉尔吉斯斯坦建设的亚洲之星农业产业合作区分别于2016年8月和2017年7月被评定为国家级境外经贸产业园区和境外农业合作示范区，受到了国家财政部、商务部、农业农村部的关注。

1. The "Going out" of Henan Agriculture

So far in Henan Province, there are 72 overseas enterprises engaging in agricultural plantation, cultivation and deep processing in 42 countries and regions in the world with a total management area (or leased land area) of over 4.5 million *mu*. Business of these enterprises is primarily divided into three types: the cultivation of grain crops and cash crops such as corn, wheat and cotton; livestock and poultry breeding along with slaughter and processing; agricultural and subsidiary products processing like edible fungi, seasoning, and so on. Apart from a number of countries along "the Belt and Road" including Tajikistan, Kyrgyzstan, Uzbekistan, Ukraine, Belarus, Cambodia, Pakistan and so on, these enterprises also have cooperation with some developed countries such as the United States, Japan and Australia as well as a few developing countries like Nigeria and Brazil. China-Tajikistan Agricultural Science-technology Demonstration Zone established by Henan Huangfanqu Industrial Group Co., Ltd. in Tajikistan has been repeatedly commended by the president of Tajikistan. Other than that, "Asian Star Agricultural Cooperation Zone" built by Henan Guiyou Industrial Group Co., Ltd. in Kyrgyzstan was respectively designated as the State-level Overseas Economic and Trade Industrial Zone and Overseas Agricultural Cooperation Demonstration Zone in August 2016 and July 2017, thus gaining attention of Ministry of Finance, Ministry of Commerce and Ministry of Agriculture and Rural Affairs of the People's Republic of China.

2. The "Bringing in" of Henan Agriculture

By the end of 2018, 286 foreign-invested enterprises related to agriculture had been set up in Henan, and multinational corporations like Charoen Pokphand Group Co., Ltd. of Thailand, Coca-Cola Company of America and so on had invested in Henan. Especially in animal husbandry, more than 20 foreign enterprises from 11 countries, including Thailand, Denmark, Germany, Australia, Japan, etc. have invested to set up 35 enterprises with a total invested capital amounting to 7.34 billion *yuan*. Business of these enterprises covers the whole industry chain of animal husbandry from feed crop cultivation, livestock and poultry breeding and raising, to livestock and poultry slaughter, processing and sale. Meanwhile, some cooperation projects, such as, China (Zhumadian) International Agricultural Products Processing Industrial Zone and Sino-Israel Science and Technology Town in Henan are in progress.

2. 河南农业引进来

截至2018年底，河南农业领域现存国（境）外投资企业286家，泰国正大、美国可口可乐等跨国公司在河南均有投资。尤其是在畜牧行业，有来自泰国、丹麦、德国、澳大利亚、日本等11个国家20多家境外企业在河南省投资农牧产业，建成农牧企业35家，总投资达73.4亿元。经营范围覆盖饲料作物种植、种畜禽繁育养殖、畜产品屠宰加工销售等畜牧业全产业链。与此同时，中国（驻马店）国际农产品加工产业园区、中以科技城等合作项目也在加速推进中。

3. 农产品出口持续向好

2016年以来，全省农产品出口总额共计446.6亿元。因地制宜培育了以鹤壁、信阳为重点区域的禽肉、茶叶基地，以南阳、三门峡为重点区域的食用菌基地，以洛阳、三门峡为重点区域的苹果基地以及以郑州、开封为重点区域的大蒜基地等产业化集群，标准化、规模化效应更加凸显，农产品出口持续向好。截至目前，河南省已经成功创建了31家国家级、120家省级出口食品农产品质量安全示范区，国家级示范区数量位居全国第二、中西部第一。

（注：本章节部分内容选自《河南日报》2017年3月9日刊登的《从"大粮仓"到"大餐桌"——培育"三农"新动能河南脚步铿锵》，作者张海涛；《河南日报》2018年6月26日刊登的《为了乡村更宜居——全省改善农村人居环境综述》，作者高长岭；《河南日报》2020年3月17日刊登的《谱写脱贫攻坚的历史性篇章》，作者归欣。）

3. The Export of Agricultural Products Keeping a Rising Trend

Since 2016, the total export volume of agricultural products has reached 44.66 billion *yuan*. Based on the local conditions, the industry cluster has been set up in Henan, including poultry raising bases and tea planting bases in Hebi and Xinyang, edible fungi cultivating bases in Nanyang and Sanmenxia, apple planting bases in Luoyang and Sanmenxia, garlic planting bases in Zhengzhou and Kaifeng. The effect of standardization and scale becomes more prominent and the export of agricultural products maintains a rising trend. So far, Henan has succeeded in setting up 31 state-level and 120 province-level Quality Safety Demonstration Zones for Exported Agricultural Products. The number of state-level demonstration zones ranks the second in China and the first in the central and western China.

(Note: Some contents of this chapter are selected from the following three articles: *From a Big Granary to a Big Dining-table, Fostering New Driving Forces for the "Three Nongs"—Agriculture, Rural Areas and Farmers*, authored by Zhang Haitao and published by *Henan Daily* on March 9, 2017, *To Make the Countryside More Livable — an Overview of the Province's Efforts to Improve the Rural Living Environment*, authored by Gao Changling and published by *Henan Daily* on June 26, 2018, and *Writing a Historic Chapter in the Fight Against Poverty*, authored by Gui Xin and published by *Henan Daily* on March 17, 2020.)

第四章

农业神话——远古深处的人文觉醒

Chapter IV

Agricultural Myths

河南，这片美丽而富饶的土地，溯自远古，伏羲在这里结网，神农在这里植谷，夏禹在这里疏淤导洪，中国人的祖先在这片沃土上耕耘、生息、繁衍，书写了一部光辉的华夏农业发展史，这里也流传着许多的神话故事和传说。当我们把这些故事串联起来，就看到一幅长长的历史画卷，栩栩如生地展示了河南农业，乃至中国农业的起源和发展，展现出中华先民探索自然规律、利用自然环境、追求与自然和谐共生的生存智慧和生存哲学。

一、燧人氏教人取火

上古时期，人们不知道火的用途，更不知道如何人工取火。有时看到自然界雷电引发的自然火，还会本能地感到恐惧，像其他动物一样飞快地逃离。后来，人们偶然在山火过后的灰烬里发现烧焦的动物尸体，闻起来有种诱人的香味，忍不住尝上一口，竟然异常美味可口，比生肉好吃多了。于是，再见到自然火时，人们不仅不再因害怕而逃离，还把自己打的猎物放进火里烧烤。慢慢地，人们又发现，冬天围在火边，就没那么冷了，而且，只要有火在身边，猛兽都不敢靠近了。人们越了解火的好处，就越想让火长燃不熄，以便随时取用。可是火种并不易保存，刮风下雨，或者看护者稍有不慎就会熄灭。

相传，有一个风姓年轻人，为了找到保存火种的方法，来到了"燧明国"。这个国度长着一棵大树，叫"燧木"。燧木长得枝繁叶茂，遮蔽了整个国家，连太阳和月亮的光辉都照不进来。这样的地方本该是暗无天日、不辨昼夜的，可是年轻人发现并非如此，因为大树的枝丫间到处闪烁着点点亮光，足够人们照明用了。再仔细观察，青年发现，有一种长着长脚爪、黑脊背、白肚子的奇特大鸟，像啄木鸟一样不停地用短而硬的喙去啄树干，每啄一下，树干就会迸发出灿烂的火花。看到这个情景，年轻人突然明白了取火的方法。于是他折下一些燧木的树枝，

On the beautiful and fertile land of Henan, our ancestors cultivated, lived and multiplied, writing a splendid agricultural history of China along with many agricultural mythologies and legends, such as Fuxi netting, Shennong planting grains, Yu the Great taming rivers and so on. These stories can be linked together into a vivid historical picture which shows not only the origin and development of agriculture in Henan and even in China, but also the survival wisdom and philosophy of our ancestors who explored the natural laws, took advantage of the natural environment, and pursued the harmonious relationship with nature.

I. Suiren Teaching People to Make Fire

In ancient times, people didn't know the function of fire. Neither did they know how to make fire. Sometimes when seeing the natural fire caused by thunder and lightning, they would instinctively feel threatened and ran away quickly as animals did. Later they found in the ash animals' dead body giving off a marvelous aroma. They could not help tasting a bit, and to their surprise, it was more delicious than raw meat. Therefore, when encountering natural fire again, they didn't run away out of fear. Instead, they grilled their prey in the fire. They also found that sitting around the fire could make them feel warmer and the fire could also keep beasts away. The more people knew the use of fire, the longer they hoped the fire to burn for their convenience. But it was hard to keep the fire burning for a long time. The fire would go out on windy or raining days, or if the keeper didn't watch it carefully.

According to a legend, a young man whose surname was Feng came to "Suiming State" in order to get a method to keep flame. In this state, there was a giant tree, Suimu, whose leaves and branches were so thick and immense that the radiance of the Sun and the Moon could not pour in. Such a place should have been in complete darkness with no division of day and night, but this young man found it was not the case. Actually, a glimmer of sparks through the branches was bright enough for local people. After further observation, he realized that an extraordinarily large bird with long claws, black back and white belly kept pecking at the trunk of the tree with its short and hard beak. Each time it pecked, the trunk would burst sparks. Seeing this, the young man suddenly knew the method

用它们去钻树干,果然也有火花迸出,但迸出的火花只有光亮,并不燃烧。后来他又用别的树枝尝试,虽然很费劲,但总算得到了能燃烧的真正的火。

年轻人把钻木取火的方法教给了大家。掌握了这种取火方法,人们随时都可以生起火来,终于不必再苦苦等待打雷带给他们天火,也不必日日守着火种唯恐它熄灭。人们感念这个发现钻木取火法的年轻人,因此叫他"燧人",即"取火者"的意思。由于燧人氏结束了人们茹毛饮血的历史,带来了华夏文明的曙光,因此他被后世奉为"火祖",位列三皇之一,被称为"燧皇"。

燧人氏钻木取火的"燧明国"就是今天的河南商丘,商丘市也因此被称为"火的故乡"。燧人氏就葬在离商丘古城不远的燧皇陵。这里保存着"中华第一火种",河南省举办重大赛事时都从这儿取火。

二、伏羲氏教人结网捕鱼

伏羲是传说中的三皇之首,中华文明的肇始者。相传,西北的雷泽是雷神的居所,雷泽附近生活着华胥族。一天,一个华胥族女子在雷泽边看到一个巨大的脚印,好奇地踩了进去,因此受孕。怀孕12年后才生下伏羲。伏羲相貌奇特,长着人的头、蛇的身子,人们都说他是雷神的儿子。伏羲后来成了部落首领,带领其部族沿黄河东移,建都于陈,即今天的河南淮阳,并在这里建立了他的功业。

相传伏羲时期,人口逐渐增多,但人们仍然以狩猎为生,没有别的生存手段,打不到猎物时,人们就不得不忍饥挨饿。作为首领的伏羲为此很发愁,苦苦思索解决办法。

一天,伏羲正沿着黄河边走边想,突然有条肥大的鲤鱼从河中跳出,随即又跃入水中,如此反复了三四次。伏羲看到后灵光一闪,河里的鱼能不能捕来吃呢?于是他跳入河中捕了一条鱼,拿回去与族人分

of making fire. He drilled the trunk with the branches, which indeed generated sparks merely without fire, otherwise the whole country would have been burned out. Later, he made a trial with branches of other trees and obtained the real fire with great efforts.

The young man told others the method of making fire. With this method, people didn't have to wait for the natural fire brought by lightning. Neither did they have to watch the fire day and night. Instead, they could light fire whenever they needed. They gave the young man a name Suiren, meaning fire maker, in gratitude for his finding of the method. Because Suirenshi ended the age of eating raw birds and animals and brought the first light to Chinese civilization, he was worshiped as "Father of Fire" and "Suihuang" (Emperor Sui), one of the three ancient Emperors.

Suiming State is now called Shangqiu in Henan Province, which is also regarded as "Hometown of the Fire". Suirenshi was buried in the Tomb of Emperor Sui, not far away from the ancient city of Shangqiu. The first fire of China is preserved in this city, and people will fetch fire here whenever there is major sports events in Henan Province.

II. Fuxi Teaching People to Net Fish

According to the legend, Fuxi was the head of the three ancient Emperors, the founder of Chinese civilization. It was said that God of Thunder dwelled in Leize in Northwest with Huaxu tribe living nearby. One day, a Huaxu girl saw a giant foot mark, and stepped into it out of curiosity. Amazingly, she became pregnant and gave birth to Fuxi after 12 years of pregnancy. Fuxi had a strange appearance with human head and snake body, and was regarded as the son of God of Thunder. When growing up, Fuxi became the head of his tribe. He led his tribe eastward along the Yellow River, and established the capital at Chen which is now called Huaiyang in Henan Province where Fuxi attained great achievements.

In Fuxi's period, people still lived on hunting though the population was gradually increasing. They had to endure hunger if they could not get prey. As the head of the tribe, Fuxi was deeply worried and cudgeled his brains for a solution.

One day, Fuxi was thinking hard while walking along the Yellow River.

享,大家都觉得味道鲜美,比猎物的肉还好吃。于是伏羲就告诉其他族人去河里捕鱼。不到半日,大家都有所收获,美美地饱餐了一顿。这样不到三日,族人都学会了捕鱼。

河里的龙王知道了,很害怕,担心这样下去,他的子民早晚要被吃光,于是找到伏羲谈条件,规定人们可以在河里捕鱼,但不能用手。伏羲答应了这个荒谬的条件,龙王暗暗高兴,以为这样人们就没办法捕鱼了。

怎么样才能不用手捕到鱼呢?伏羲又开始苦苦思索。一天,伏羲正在树荫下出神地想办法,一抬头,看见一只蜘蛛在树上织网,网织好后蜘蛛就躲到树叶后,等到网里困住了不少小飞虫,蜘蛛才不慌不忙地出来饱餐一顿。伏羲茅塞顿开。于是他模仿蜘蛛,用绳编了一张网,把网放进河里,不一会儿网里就有了动静,提起来一看,里面欢蹦乱跳的都是鱼儿,比用手捕捞效果还好。伏羲赶紧把结网捕鱼的方法教给了大家。从此,人们再也不用担心没吃的了,这也是中国原始渔业的开端。

见此情景,龙王干着急却也没有办法再阻止人们捕鱼,急得眼睛都鼓了出来,所以,在中国的雕塑和绘画中,龙的眼睛都是往外鼓的。

后来人们不仅用网捕鱼虾,还用网捉飞禽、擒走兽。用网捕获的猎

伏羲
Fuxi

Chapter IV Agricultural Myths

Suddenly a large carp jumped out of the river, then into the river. It repeated this action three or four times. Inspired by this, Fuxi suddenly got the idea of catching fish to eat. Then he jumped into the river and got one. Anyone who tasted it thought it was more delicious than their prey. Accordingly, Fuxi told others to catch fish in the river. Less than half a day, all people caught some fish and had a full stomach. Within less than three days, people in the tribe learned to catch fish.

The Dragon King in the river got this news and felt fearful. Worrying that the fish in the river would have been eaten up, the Dragon King went to negotiate with Fuxi, ruling that they could catch fish in the river on condition that they did not use their hands. Fuxi accepted this ridiculous requirement, while the Dragon King was glad in secret, believing that people could not catch fish without using their hands.

Fuxi kept thinking hard about how to catch fish without using hands. One day, he was sitting under a tree, musing over this problem. Looking up, he accidentally saw a spider weaving a web. After its work done, the spider hid itself behind the leaves waiting for little bugs to get trapped in the web, and then had a good meal. Suddenly enlightened by this, Fuxi knitted a net and threw it into the river. For a while, there was a stir in the net. He lifted it and saw a lot of lively fish in his net. This method was much more efficient than catching fish with hands. Fuxi taught people how to weave net and how to fish with it. Since then, people didn't have to worry about food. This is the beginning of primitive fishery in China.

This annoyed the Dragon King who had no way to stop people from netting fish. He was so anxious that his eyes bulged out. That's why dragons are popeyed in Chinese sculptures and paintings.

Later, the net was used not only to catch fish and shrimps, but also to trap birds and animals. People usually trapped living preys and sometimes more than necessary. Fuxi began thinking about raising these living animals for future eating. So he taught people to pen the living preys and let them reproduce offspring. These penned animals gradually lost their wildness and turned into domestic fowl and livestock. Since then, people didn't have to go hunting every day, because they had secure food resources.

物通常是活的，有时捕多了吃不完，伏羲又想，把这些猎物喂养起来，不就是将来的食物吗？于是，他又教人们圈养猎物，让它们生育繁殖，久而久之，这些动物脱去了野性，变成了家禽、家畜。从此，人们不必天天出去打猎，食物来源也有了保障。

三、炎帝教人耕作

炎帝是继伏羲之后中华民族的又一个人文始祖。他生长在姜水（今陕西岐水）边，因此姓姜。和伏羲一样，他在历代神话中也是半人半兽的神人，长着牛首人身。

炎帝又称神农氏，在中原神话中，他既是火神和谷神，也是太阳神，是中华农耕文明的开创者。

炎帝时期，相传有一天，一只红色的神鸟从天空飞过，嘴里衔着一棵长着9个穗的谷子，有些谷粒掉落到地上，炎帝就把这些谷粒收集起来当种子，教人们播种，到了秋天便收获了更多的谷粒。人们觉得，与其每天四处奔波，去野外采集和打猎，还不如固定在一个地方种庄稼，于是就逐渐定居下来，开始了春种秋收的农耕生活。

虽然人工取火是燧人氏的功劳，然而推广火的应用，尤其是将火应用于农业生产的却是炎帝。炎帝按照火的不同用途，将火分为几大类，如照明的烛火、取暖的堂火、烹煮食物的灶火等。他设专人负责取火、存火、掌火和用火，这样既能充分利用火，造福民众，又大大降低了火灾隐患。

随着部落的发展壮大，人口越来越多，需要更多的土地种植庄稼，以满足人们吃饭的需求。炎帝就亲自带领部族开荒种地。开垦荒地的第一步当然是除去蔓生的杂草和树木。过去都是人工砍伐，这样既耗时又费力。一次，雷电引发了山火，大火过处一片焦土，炎帝突然想到了一种最好的垦荒办法——用火烧，这样不仅省时省力，杂草灌木燃烧后的

III. Yan Emperor Teaching People to Plant Grains

Yan Emperor, just after Fuxi, is another founder of Chinese civilization. He was born and grew up near Jiangshui River (now Qishui of Shaanxi Province) with Jiang as his surname. Just like Fuxi, he was also a god with the appearance of half human and half animal, that is, he had an ox head and a human body.

Yan Emperor, also called Shennong, is regarded as the god of agriculture, fire and the sun, as well as the founder of agricultural civilization in China.

Legend has it that one day in the period of Yan Emperor, a red holy bird was flying in the sky holding a grain with nine ears in its mouth. Some of the seeds fell down to the earth which were collected and sewed into the field by Yan Emperor. People harvested more grains in autumn. Consequently, they preferred to stay in a fixed place to plant crops rather than to hunt in the wilderness. Then they decided to settle down and started their farming life in which they sewed in spring and harvested in autumn.

It was Suirenshi who discovered how to make fire, but it was Yan Emperor who popularized the use of fire, especially the use of fire in agriculture. According to the different uses of the fire, Yan Emperor divided fire into several kinds, such as, candle fire for lighting, hall fire for getting warmth, stove fire for cooking, and so on. Specially-assigned persons were responsible for making fire, keeping fire, and using fire respectively, which could not only make use of fire to benefit people, but also to reduce disasters caused by fire.

As the tribe developed with an increasingly larger population, people needed more lands to plant crops in order to meet their need for food. Yan Emperor himself led his people to cultivate virgin land for farming. The first step was to log off wild bushes and woods. They used to do it with hands, which took much time and energy. Once a fire caused by thunder scorched everything in the mountain, which inspired Yan Emperor to cultivate virgin land by burning. This turned out to be a good method. On the one hand, it saved a lot of time and efforts; on the other hand, the plant ash turned into good fertilizer which could promote the growth of the crops. Later, after harvesting, peasants directly burn the straws in the field to supplement the fertility of the soil. This farming method has been

草木灰还是上好的肥料,更有利于作物的生长。后来,农民将收获后的秸秆也就地焚烧,用来补充土壤消耗的肥力。这一耕作方法在中国一直沿用了几千年。

用火烧虽然可以轻松除去地表的杂草和树木,但草根和树根还留在地下,不清除干净,不仅难以播种,来年还会再长出来,与作物争夺空间和水肥,庄稼还是长不好。于是,炎帝发明了掘地翻土用的工具——耒耜,也就是犁的前身。他教人们用木制的耒耜翻地松土,大大提高了耕作的效率。等庄稼成熟了,他又教人们用蚌壳制成的镰刀收割庄稼。相比之前使用的简陋石制农具,炎帝发明的耒耜和蚌镰,携带和使用起来更轻便,当然也极大地提高了生产效率。

宁静而美丽的小城淮阳市不仅有个规模宏大的太昊陵,在县城西北5公里处还有个闻名遐迩的五谷台,相传炎帝就是在这里教民稼穑。附近还有个神农井,据传是炎帝挖的,用来教人们汲水浇灌五谷。后来人们确实在这里发掘出了新石期时代的石锛、石镰和石斧,因此,炎帝可能并非只存在于神话传说中。

太昊陵
Taihao Tomb

passed down from generation to generation.

The wild plants and bushes on the surface could be cleaned away by burning, but their roots were still left in the earth which made sewing difficult. And they could regrow next year and affected the growth of crops by consuming space, water and fertilizer. Therefore, Yan Emperor invented "Leisi"— a kind of tilling tool to dig and turn soil, which was the predecessor of plough. He taught people to turn and loosen the soil with wooden Leisi. This method greatly improved their cultivation. In the harvesting season, Yan Emperor taught people to reap with clam sickles. Compared with simple stone tools, Leisi and clam sickle were convenient to carry and use, thus greatly improving the farming efficiency.

Apart from the glorious Taihao Tomb, Wugu Temple is another famous historic site in Huaiyang. It was said to be the place where Yan Emperor, also known as Shennong, taught people to plant "Wugu" (five grains—broomcorn millet, millet, bean, wheat and rice). Shennong Well nearby was said to be drilled by Yan Emperor who taught people to fetch water to irrigate crops. Stone adze, stone sickle and stone axe in the Neolithic Age were right discovered here. Thereupon, Yan Emperor may not be a figure only in the myth.

Apart from Wugu Temple and Shennong Well in Huaiyang, Shennong Mountain in Qinyang City is also well-known to the locals with many tales of Shennong. Moreover, many place names in the mountain are related to Shennong, such as Baicao Slope, Shizu Peak, Shennong Altar, Yizu Temple and so on.

IV. Yellow Emperor Establishing Chinese Calendar

Yellow Emperor who was after Yan Emperor, was the head of the united tribes along the Yellow River. It was said that Yan Emperor and Yellow Emperor were relatives, both coming from the Shaodian clan and being the heads of their tribes respectively. Later, the tribe of Yan Emperor declined while the tribe of Yellow Emperor became stronger. Yellow Emperor led his troops to fight with Chiyou tribe in the South. He defeated Chiyou tribe and then the tribe of Yan Emperor, uniting all tribes in the Central Plains, and becoming the emperor of the united tribes accordingly. He established his capital in Youxiong (now Xinzheng in Henan Province). That is why Yellow Emperor is also called Youxiongshi. As an

除了淮阳的五谷台和神农井，河南沁阳还有座神农山，当地流传着许多关于神农的神话故事。山上的地名也多与神农有关，比如百草坡、始祖峰、神农坛、医祖庙等。

四、黄帝制定历法

黄帝是黄河流域最著名的部落联盟首领。相传黄帝和炎帝是近亲，都出自少典氏家族，也都是各自部落的首领。后来，炎帝部落逐渐衰落，黄帝部落则日渐强盛。黄帝率部与南方的蚩尤部族大战，打败了蚩尤，后又打败了炎帝，统一了中原各部落，成为天下的共主，定都有熊，即今河南新郑，故黄帝亦称"有熊氏"。作为战无不胜的大英雄，黄帝受到后人的无比推崇，他的子孙众多，不断繁衍，逐渐成为华夏族的主体，因此，黄帝被尊为华夏族的始祖。由于炎帝和黄帝原本就是近亲，后来他们的部落又融合在一起，因此，中国人常常称自己是"炎黄子孙"。

黄帝时期涌现了许多发明创造，涵盖了衣食住行各个方面以及政治、经济、商业各个领域。虽然这些发明创造并非都是黄帝本人的功劳，但出于对黄帝的崇拜，人们都归功于黄帝，因此，黄帝成了一个无所不能、无所不会的"大发明家"，就如同《圣经》中记载的创造万事万物的上帝一样。在这些发明创造中，与河南农业关系最为紧密的就是历法的制定。

相传，黄帝打败蚩尤，平定天下后，非常重视农业发展，派专人指导农事。那时，农耕活动虽然已经比较普遍，但人们并没有清晰的时间观念，只是凭感觉，大致按照四季更替进行耕作，这样往往会错过最关键的播种、施肥、收获等时间节点，收成自然也大受影响。为了解决这个问题。黄帝设专人观测日、月、星辰的运行规律，并依据观测结果推演、制定了历法，同时划分了四季，设立了节令。这样一来，大家按

invincible hero, along with his large amount of descendants who constituted the main body of the Chinese nation, Yellow Emperor is worshipped as the founder of the Chinese nation. Since Yan Emperor and Yellow Emperor were relatives and their tribes were united as one, Chinese people always call themselves "Descendants of Yan Emperor and Yellow Emperor".

In the age of Yellow Emperor, there appeared a lot of inventions, covering basic necessities of life and all fields in politics, economy and business. Although not all those inventions were made by Yellow Emperor himself, people attributed them to him out of their worship. Therefore, Yellow Emperor became a "Great Inventor" who was almighty and could do everything, just like Almighty God in the *Bible* who created everything in the Universe. Of all these inventions, the establishment of calendar is closely connected with agriculture in Henan.

According to the folklore, after defeating Chiyou tribe and having a state at peace, Yellow Emperor attached so much importance to the development of agriculture that he specially assigned persons to supervise farming. Although farming was widespread at that time, people didn't have a clear idea of when to plant. They just followed their sense to farm roughly in accordance with four seasons. As a result, they often missed the critical time for sewing, applying fertilizer and harvesting, which seriously reduced their yields. In order to solve this problem, Yellow Emperor specially appointed persons to watch the changing positions of the sun, the moon and the stars. Based on their observation, they deduced and established a calendar in which a year was divided into four seasons, each having its solar terms. Thus, people could timely farm according to the solar terms. For example, they began spring ploughing after "Beginning of Spring", applying fertilizer around "Rain Water", harvesting immediately after "Grain in Ear", and so on. In short, with such a calendar, people could systematically arrange their farming, which pushed agricultural civilization a great leap forward.

The birthplace and the capital of Yellow Emperor lies in Xinzheng where there are more than ten relics related to him. So a grand ancestor worship ceremony in honor of Yellow Emperor is annually held here. This great ceremony has been attracting Chinese people all over the world to worship the common ancestor.

The giant statues of Yan Emperor and Yellow Emperor are standing at the

照节令的提示,"立春"后开始春耕,"雨水"时勤给作物施肥,"芒种"后抓紧收割……总之,有了历法,人们就可以有条不紊地安排农事活动,农耕文明又向前迈了一大步。

新郑是黄帝的家乡和故都,因此,这一带有10余处黄帝遗迹。每年这里都要举办黄帝故里拜祖大典。黄帝故里拜祖大典已经成了河南省的重大节庆,吸引着大量海内外华人前来拜谒这位共同的祖先。

郑州市的黄河岸边伫立着炎黄二帝的巨型雕塑。巨塑背依邙山,俯瞰黄河,以同盟山山体为炎黄二帝之身,整体高达106米,比美国自由女神像高8米,可说是"地球第一雕"。巨塑内部是展厅,介绍炎黄二帝的丰功伟绩。巨塑前是宽阔的炎黄广场。此处已成为亿万炎黄子孙寻根拜祖的圣地。

河南灵宝市区西20千米的荆山上亦有一处黄帝遗存,叫铸鼎塬,据说是黄帝铸鼎升仙之处。此处建有黄帝陵,供后人瞻仰拜谒。奇特的是,在铸鼎塬周围8千米的范围内,考古人员发现了20余处仰韶文化遗址,似乎证明了黄帝存在的真实性。

炎黄二帝巨塑
The statues of Yan Emperor and Yellow Emperor

bank of the Yellow River in Zhengzhou. The statues stand against Mangshan Mountain, facing the Yellow River, 106 meters high, 8 meters higher than the Statue of Liberty of America. So it can be called "The First Statue of the World". The inside of the statue is a hall exhibiting the achievements of the two emperors. In front of the statue is Yan-Huang Square which has become a holy place for Chinese people to trace their ancestry and worship their ancestors.

On Jingshan Mountain, 20 kilometers west to Lingbao, Henan Province, there is a relic of Yellow Emperor, called Zhuding Yuan. It was said to be the place where Yellow Emperor cast tripod in order to become immortal. A mausoleum of Yellow Emperor was built here for people to worship. Oddly enough, within 8 kilometers around Zhuding Yuan, more than 20 relics of Yangshao culture were discovered, which seemed to prove the real existence of Yellow Emperor in history.

V. Leizu Teaching People to Raise Silkworm

China is the country of silk, the first civilization in the world to domesticate wild silkworms and make artificial silk. According to records and archaeological findings, Chinese silk was delivered to Greece as early as the 5th Century BC and greatly appreciated by the Greek upper-class. Since the exact name of this silk-producing Eastern country was unknown, China was named "Seres" at that time, meaning "Country of Silk". It is said that Julius Caesar once went to the theater in a gorgeous silk gown which attracted the eyeballs of all the audience. Historically, European royalty and the rich used to be fond of Chinese silk, cherishing it as a treasure.

Having been an important part of Chinese agriculture since ancient times, the mulberry planting and silkworms domesticating, together with farming, are called "farming and sericulture". According to the myths of the Central Plains, sericulture originated from Leizu, Xilingshi's daughter, who was born in Xiping County, Henan Province. As wife of Yellow Emperor, she assisted him to unify the Central Plains, nurtured the people as an empress, did sericulture and wove clothes. She is worshiped by the descendants as the "Goddess of Silkworm".

At that time, women were mainly in charge of collecting wild fruits and weaving clothing for clothes. One day, Leizu led the women in her tribe picking

五、嫘祖教人养蚕

中国是丝绸之国，也是世界上最早驯养野蚕、人工制丝的国家。根据文献记载和考古发现，最迟在公元前5世纪，中国的丝绸已经传到希腊，深受希腊上层社会喜爱。由于不知道这个出产丝绸的东方国度的确切名称，于是希腊人把中国叫作"赛里斯"（Seres），即"丝之国"。据说凯撒大帝曾穿着一件华美的丝绸长袍去看戏，引得全场观众围观与赞叹。历史上，欧洲各国的贵族和富人也一直对中国丝绸青睐有加，视之为无上珍品。

植桑养蚕自古就是中国农业的一个重要组成部分，和种植业一起并称为"农桑"。根据中原流传的神话，养蚕是从嫘祖开始的。相传，嫘祖是西陵氏之女，出生在河南省西平县，是黄帝的元妃。她辅助黄帝统一中原，母仪天下，养蚕制衣，被后人奉为"蚕神"。

那时，妇女的主要职责是采集野果和织布制衣。一天，嫘祖带领部落里的妇女上山摘野果，她们一连爬了三座山，却没采到多少果子。她们泄气了，都坐下休息，只有嫘祖擦了把头上的汗，爬上了第四座山。在山坡上，她看到很多绿油油的树，树上结满了白亮亮的果子，于是采满了一大筐带回家。可是这些外表漂亮的果子怎么也咬不动。嫘祖想，也许需要煮煮才能吃，于是她把果子倒进锅里煮。不承想，煮过以后果子变成了滑溜溜的线一般的东西。嫘祖有些沮丧，转而去缝补衣物。恰好缝衣服的线用完了，嫘祖突发奇想，从锅里捞起一条"白线"，穿在了骨针上。不料这些"线"柔韧结实，十分好用。她很高兴，就把锅里的"线"都捞出来晾干，织成布，给黄帝做了一件新衣服。黄帝穿上这件衣服后感觉又软又轻又滑，十分舒服，问嫘祖这是用什么做的，嫘祖高兴地讲述了自己的奇遇和发现。

为了让其他族人也穿上这样的衣服，嫘祖再次上山采白果，却发

wild fruits in the mountain. They did not get many fruits after climbing three mountains. Tired and discouraged, they all sat down for a rest except Leizu. She wiped sweat off her forehead and climbed up the fourth mountain. There on the hillside, she found many green trees with bright white fruits. She took back home a full basket of such fruits. Beautiful as they were, the white fruits were too hard to chew. She thought maybe they could be edible after being boiled, so she poured them into a pot with boiling water. Unexpectedly, the boiled fruits turned into smooth threadlike objects. Leizu was a little frustrated and turned to mend clothes. When she ran out of the sewing thread, Leizu suddenly got the idea of using the "threads" in the pot instead. She picked up one piece, and put it through the eye of the bone needle. Much to her surprise, the "threads" were pliable and tough, and perfectly suitable for mending clothes. She got them out and dried them with excitement. She knitted cloth with them and made a new dress for Yellow Emperor. Feeling quite comfortable in this soft, light and smooth clothes, he asked Leizu what it was made of. Leizu explained to him her miraculous encounter and incidental discovery happily.

To make it accessible to other people in her tribe, Leizu went back to pick the white fruit in the mountain, only to find that there was a hole in the top of each white fruit, and many gray moths flew all over. After she boiled the fruit with holes, she found that the pot was full of short threads, too short to be woven. Without being discouraged, Leizu went there again the following spring, and found the trees covered by grey-white fat worms that fed on the green leaves. A few days later, the worms began to spit out thin silk thread to wrap them up, and consequently, the trees were "bearing" beautiful white fruits once more. She suddenly realized that these fruits were "homes" for the worms. After two years' careful observation, Leizu had a thorough understanding of their growth habits and learned how to raise them. She named them "silkworms" and the trees "mulberry trees". Then she taught women to plant mulberry, to raise silkworm, to pick cocoon, to reel silk and to brocade in silk. Thereafter, China has had a light, soft and smooth silk fabric. Thus, Leizu is regarded as the ancestor of the sericulture industry and also wins the name of "Goddess of Silkworm".

There are many legends and relics about Leizu in Henan Province. For instance, in her hometown Xiping County, you can find such relics as Xiling

现每个白果的顶端都有一个破洞,满山飞着一种灰色的蛾子。她把这种带洞的白果采回家,煮过后,满锅都是碎线头,没法织布。嫘祖并不气馁。第二年春天,她再次上山,发现树上爬满胖胖的灰白色虫子,这些虫子以绿油油的树叶为食。又过了些日子,这些虫子开始吐出细细的丝线把自己包裹起来,于是树上又"结满"了她见过的漂亮白果子。嫘祖恍然大悟,原来这些果子是虫子的"家"。又细心观察了两年,嫘祖彻底了解了这些虫子的生长习性,知道了如何饲养它们,她给这些虫子起名叫"蚕",养蚕的树叫"桑树",并开始带领妇女们栽桑、养蚕、采茧、缫丝和织锦。从此,中国就有了又轻又软、光滑无比的丝绸织物了。后人把嫘祖奉为养蚕业的始祖,尊她为"蚕神"。

河南省有许多关于嫘祖的传说和遗迹,仅她的家乡西平县境内就有西陵亭、嫘祖庙、嫘坟、九女山等。嫘祖庙每年农历三月三举行盛大的庙会,持续7天,庙会期间人们唱大戏、祭嫘祖,人山人海,热闹非凡。此外,黄帝故里新郑每年也举办嫘祖纪念节,开封和荥阳等地也都有纪念嫘祖的庙宇。由此可见,当年嫘祖的足迹遍布河南。除此之外,农家妇女们还把嫘祖的像供奉在她们放织布机的房里,以示对嫘祖的尊崇。

六、后稷教人辨识五谷

后稷是炎帝之后又一个对农业发展做出重大贡献的人,被尊为"谷神"。

后稷生活在尧舜时期,相传他是"大地之神"姜嫄之子。后稷出生后,屡次被丢弃。第一次他被丢在狭窄的小巷里,但是经过的牛马竟然都绕开他走。第二次被丢在树林里,刚好林中有许多人,把他捡了回来。第三次被丢在冰封的河沟上,结果一群鸟飞来,纷纷用鸟羽覆盖他,以免他冻伤。一个尚在襁褓中的婴儿能屡次大难不死,预示着他日

Pavilion, Leizu Temple, Leizu Tomb, and Jiunü Mountain, etc. An annual grand temple fair on the third day of the third lunar month in Leizu Temple usually lasts for seven days, during which people sing operas and offer sacrifices to Leizu. In Xinzheng City, the hometown of Yellow Emperor, the memorial festival in honor of Leizu is also held every year. The temples in honor of Leizu can also be found in many other cities like Kaifeng and Xingyang, which implies that she travelled all over Henan Province. What's more, female villagers also enshrined her statue in their loom rooms to show their respect for her.

VI. Houji Teaching People to Identify Five Grains

Another great contributor to the development of agriculture after Yan Emperor is Houji who is honored as "God of Grains".

Houji lived in time of Emperor Yao and Emperor Shun. Legend says that he was the son of Jiang Yuan, God of the Earth. Soon after he was born, he was repeatedly abandoned by his mother. When he was deserted in a narrow alley for the first time, the passing cattle and horses all bypassed him. When he was abandoned in the forest for the second time, there happened to be a lot of people in the woods who picked him up. When he was thrown on the icy ditch for the third time, a flock of birds flew in and protected him with their feathers. The fact that an infant in its cradle could survive many crises foretold his future extraordinary experience and achievements.

At that time, farming activities were common, but the low yields could not meet people's demand for food due to single crop planting and backward farming techniques.

Houji was extremely interested in and gifted for farming from his childhood. He loved collecting the wild plant seeds and planting them in the soil. Through trial and error, he succeeded in cultivating new crops, including broomcorn millet, millet, wheat, beans and rice, collectively called "Wugu". In agricultural practice, he also developed a set of unique farming techniques, so whatever he planted, he would gain a good harvest. The villagers admired him deeply and learned from him attentively. He taught them all about how to select seeds, remove weeds and fertilize the soil to improve yields. In this way, he gradually became so well-known

后不凡的经历和成就。

那时候，虽然农耕活动已经比较普遍，但种植的作物比较单一，耕作技术也很落后，因此产量不高，无法满足人们对粮食的需求。

后稷自幼在耕种方面有很大的兴趣，也极有天赋。他喜欢采集野生植物的种子，把它们种在地里。通过不断尝试，他成功地培育出了新的农作物种类，包括麻、黍、稷、麦、豆等，统称为"五谷"。在农业实践中，他还摸索出了一套独特的耕作技术，因此，不管他种什么，总是长势喜人，他种的大豆长得茂盛，种的谷子谷粒饱满，种的小麦麦穗沉甸甸地下垂，种的瓜果硕果累累……乡亲们都很佩服他，纷纷向他取经。他也毫无保留，悉数向人们传授如何选种、除草和施肥。就这样，他渐渐声名远播，连尧帝都听闻了他的事迹，于是请他做农师，掌管全国的农业生产。

作为农师，他还对土地进行考察，划定田界，评定耕地的优劣等级，以便更合理有效地利用土地，同时继续带领大家开辟新田，以养活日益增多的民众。

后稷还是最早在田里开挖沟渠的人。他把两架犁并在一起，在田里开出宽一尺、深一尺的沟，称为"田沟"，方便了农业灌溉和排涝。

除了教人们种五谷，后稷还教人们种植苎麻，生产麻线，用来织布制衣。

由于功劳巨大，后稷被后世尊为"谷神"。

七、大禹疏导治水

水是生命之源，也是农业的根本。没有水，作物无法生长；水太多，作物也无法成活。因此，如何利用水灌溉农田，同时防治洪涝灾害，成为原始农业必须面对和解决的问题。由于黄河从境内穿过，河南有幸成为中华民族和华夏文明的发祥地。然而黄河在给先人们提供滋养

that even Emperor Yao heard of him and invited him officially to take charge of the country's farming.

As a farming official, Houji also investigated the land, demarcated the field boundary, and assessed the grades of arable land so as to make better use of land. At the same time, he continued to open up new fields with the people in order to feed the growing population.

Houji was also the first person to excavate ditches in the fields. He put two ploughs together to dig a trench, called "field ditch", one foot wide and one foot deep, which facilitated agricultural irrigation and drainage.

Besides teaching people to grow Wugu, Houji also guided people to grow ramie and make ramie thread for weaving clothes.

Houji, with his great contributions, was honored as "God of Grains".

VII. Yu the Great Taming Rivers

Water is the source of life, and also indispensable for agriculture. Crops can not grow where water is too scarce or too much. Therefore, the severe problem that primitive agriculture had to face and solve was how to irrigate farmland and how to control floods at the same time. Henan has the honor of being the birthplace of Chinese nation and civilization, as the Yellow River passes through its territory. However, the Yellow River, while providing resources to our ancestors, also became the cause of their disasters due to frequent floods. Since ancient times, our forefathers have been devoting themselves to floods control. As a result, many mythologies about water control have been passed down. The most famous one is "Yu the Great Taming Rivers".

Speaking of "Yu the Great Taming Rivers", we need mention his father Gun's flood controlling experience. Legend has it that during the period of Emperors Yao and Shun, not only countless fertile fields were flooded and crops ruined, but also the beasts were rampant. Homeless people had to hide in mountains and on giant trees to avoid the flood. Emperor Yao ordered Gun to solve it. Gun adopted "blocking" method to build dams everywhere in an effort to harness the water inside. Although the dams temporarily worked, the increasing floods eventually broke them through, which made the flooding monster become more fierce and

的同时，也因水患频发而成为灾难的源头。从远古时期开始，中国人的祖先就致力于治理水患，也因此流传下来不少治水的神话，其中最著名的当数大禹治水的故事。

说到大禹治水，就不得不先说说大禹的父亲鲧的治水经历。相传尧舜时期，洪水泛滥，无数良田被淹，地里庄稼尽毁，地上凶禽猛兽横行，百姓流离失所，不得不躲避在高山和大树上，苦不堪言。尧帝命鲧治水，鲧采用"堵"的方式，在各处建大坝，试图拦截洪水。堤坝虽然暂时拦截了洪水，却使洪水越聚越多，最终冲破堤坝，变得越发凶猛，危害也更大。鲧努力了9年，地面上依然是洪水肆虐，民不聊生。舜继位后，责怪鲧治水不力，杀了鲧。鲧虽然被砍了头，但天下洪水未治，他心有不甘，尸体3年不腐。鲧用全部的精血孕育了一个生命，一个可以帮他完成治水使命的英雄人物——大禹。

禹一出生就已经成年，他向天帝请命治水，以完成父亲鲧的遗愿。禹总结父亲治水失败的教训，他认识到，堵的方法不可行，治水只能另寻他法。经过仔细观察思考，禹决定采用疏导的方法，通过河道将洪水引到大海里去，从而彻底解决水患问题。他去找应龙帮忙疏导河川。应龙走在前面，用他的尾巴在大地上画出九条大河的走向。禹就率领众人跟在应龙后面开凿河道，这样就形成了中国现在的大江大河。

这一天，禹治黄河到了河南，发现一座大山挡住了河道，他用神力挥剑将大山砍成了三段，好像劈开了三道门，使滔滔河水得以分流而过，这个地方就是现在的三门峡，至今还留有禹王治水的遗迹。

还有一次禹治水到了轘辕山，这是河南偃师东南的一座高山，山势险峻。禹需要打通这座山，使洪水顺利通过。禹和他的妻子涂山娇约定，他在山里干活，饿了就敲鼓让妻子送饭。为了尽快打通大山，禹变成一只大黑熊，用他的嘴和利爪凿山开路。有一天，他正干得起劲，利爪扒落的石块碰巧打在鼓上，发出"咚咚"的声音。听到鼓声，涂山娇以为丈夫饿了，急急忙忙做好了饭送进山里，却看到一头熊正在拼命地

more harmful. After nine years' hard work, things remained unchanged. After Shun succeeded the throne, he blamed Gun for his failure in controlling floods and killed him. Although Gun was beheaded, the disaster continued. Strangely his body hadn't become rotten for three years. Finally Gun gave birth to a son with all his essence and blood, a hero — Yu the Great, who could help him complete the mission of flood control.

A born adult, Yu asked the Emperor of Heaven to delegate him to control water so that he could complete his father's last wish. Summing up the lessons from his father's failure, Yu realized that the blocking method was not feasible. Through careful observation and reflection, he adopted method of diversion to lead floods to the sea through the rivers, thus eradicating the problem. He went to Yinglong (a winged dragon) for help to channel the rivers. After Yinglong drew the direction of nine major rivers on the earth with his tail, Yu led the people to follow Yinglong's instruction to excavate rivers, thus making nowadays rivers in China.

One day, when Yu was trying to control the Yellow River in Henan, he found a high mountain blocking the way. He cut the mountain into three sections with a sword. It seemed that he had opened three doors to allow the water to flow separately. This is where the city now we call Sanmenxia locates. There are still relics of Yu the Great taming rivers.

Yu once arrived at the steep Huanyuan Mountain in the southeast of Yanshi, Henan Province, where he had to tunnel this mountain for the flood. He told his wife Tushan Jiao to send food to him whenever he signaled with drum sound. So when he was hungry, he would drum. In order to get through the mountain as soon as possible, Yu turned into a big black bear and chiseled the mountain with his teeth and claws. He was working so hard that he did not notice the fallen stones beating the drum and making the sound. Thinking he was hungry, his wife rushed to make a meal and sent it to the mountain. However, she saw a bear desperately chiseling the mountain. She got shocked how come she had married a bear! She shouted and ran away angrily. Realizing that his wife misunderstood him, Yu rushed to chase her in such a hurry that he forgot to convert himself back into a human being. She kept running with the bear chasing her, all the way to the foot of Songshan Mountain in Dengfeng City, Henan Province, until there

扒呀拱呀。涂山娇想不到自己竟然嫁给了一头熊，又惊又气，大叫一声回身就跑。禹这才看到涂山娇，知道妻子误会了，就赶忙去追她，可他却忘记变回人形。涂山娇看到黑熊追来，跑得更快了。就这样一个跑一个追，一直跑到河南登封的嵩山脚下，涂山娇看到无路可逃，又急又怕，变成了石头。禹知道涂山娇已经怀孕，看到妻子变成了石头，急得大叫："还我儿子！"石头突然裂开，生出了一个男婴，禹给他取名"启"，就是"裂开"的意思。

为了治水，禹带领众人没日没夜地干，他甚至三次路过家门而不入，不愿意为了私事耽误了治水的大事。虽为部落首领，他却和大家一样，风里来雨里去，皮肤黝黑，穿着蓑衣，戴着斗笠，手拿木耒。大家都被他这种公而忘私的行为感动了，干起活来异常卖力。就这样经过了13个春秋，禹终于带领大家疏通了所有的河道，洪水彻底退了，被淹没的田地露了出来，人们又能够过上春种秋收、安居乐业的太平日子了。为了表达对禹的感激，人们一致拥戴他做部落联盟的领袖，尊称他为"大禹"。

八、酿酒始祖杜康

酒出自粮食，是人们对粮食深加工的产物。中国是曲酒的发源地，而最早酿酒的中国人是杜康，他酿的酒被后人称为"杜康酒"。

相传，杜康家住河南洛阳一带。因善于农事，他被黄帝任命为农师，指导大家耕作。在他的努力下，粮食连年大丰收，得到了黄帝的称赞。在大家庆祝丰收的时候，负责保管粮食的首领却发了愁，因为太多的粮食堆积在粮仓里，时间一久就发霉长芽了。黄帝知道了这事，认为是那个首领不尽职尽责，免除了他的职务，让杜康兼管粮食储存。杜康仔细观察后，发现粮食发霉长芽是因为淋雨受潮了。他苦思冥想，终于想出个好办法：把大树的树干掏空，将粮食存放在树干

was no way to escape. Being anxious and afraid, she turned herself into a stone. Yu knew that his wife was pregnant, so he shouted: "Give back my son!" The stone suddenly split and gave birth to a baby boy. Yu named him "Qi" which means "split".

To dredge the rivers, Yu led his people to work day and night. He was so dedicated that he refrained from going back home three times when passing by. A tribal leader as he was, he suffered and sacrificed a lot as everyone else. Dark skin, in sedge, wearing a bamboo hat, wood tool in hand, Yu worked in all grave weathers. Everyone was deeply moved by his sacrificing conduct and worked extremely hard. So after 13 years, they finally succeeded in dredging all the rivers, with floods completely retreated and fields exposed. Therefore, people could do farm work and live a good life in peace. In order to thank Yu, people unanimously embraced him as the leader of the tribal alliance and honored him as "Yu the Great".

VIII. Du Kang — Father of Wine Making

Wine is brewed out of grains, the products of deep grain processing. China is the birthplace of yeast liquor, with Du Kang as the first Chinese to make wine. So this wine is called "Du Kang Wine".

It was said that Du Kang lived in Luoyang, Henan Province. Being expert at farming work, he was appointed by Yellow Emperor as a farming official, instructing others to plant. Under his guidance, farmers had years of continuous harvest. Du Kang was praised by Yellow Emperor accordingly. When people celebrated the harvest, the head who was in charge of the grain storage became worried, because the grains would mold and sprout if they were piled in the barn for a long time. This was known by Yellow Emperor who believed that he didn't fulfill his duty. Thus the head was discharged, and Du Kang was appointed to this post instead. After a careful observation, Du Kang found that the grains molded and sprouted just because they were caught by rain. He thought and thought, and finally came up with a good idea: dig a hollow in the trunk of the tree and store the grains there. A year later, the trees in which the grains were stored sent out a kind of fragrance, and the trunks leaked watery liquid which tasted sweet

酒神杜康
God of wine —Du Kang

  里,这样就不怕被淋湿了。然而,一年之后,储藏粮食的树林中散发出了浓郁而奇特的香气,树干上还渗出了水一样的液体,尝起来甘甜爽口,香味浓郁。杜康打开树洞查看,发现储存在里面的高粱都变了样,成了浸泡在一汪清澈液体中的废渣。杜康惊呆了,不知道该如何向黄帝交代。这时,一个猎户告诉他,这些奇特的"神水"好喝又提神,喝完后不仅让人烦恼尽消,浑身还有使不完的劲儿。杜康半信半疑地喝了一碗,发现果然如老人所言。于是,杜康壮起胆子带了些"神水"给黄帝,黄帝喝完后也连声称赞,不仅没有怪罪杜康,反而命令杜康专门负责将多余的粮食制作成这种"神水",用来祭祀天地和祖宗,以保佑人们平安顺遂,他还让负责造字的仓颉给这种液体取名叫"酒"。从此,酒成了最重要的祭品之一。

  后来,人们又发现了酒的很多妙处。适当饮酒,不仅有利于健康,还可以治病。饮酒可以使人精神振奋,增长勇气,因此,壮士出征前往

and pleasant. Opening up the hollow, Du Kang found that the sorghum in it had turned into dregs immerged in a pool of clear liquid. He was shocked and didn't know how to explain it to Yellow Emperor. At that moment, a hunter told him that this tasty "magical water" could dispel one's worries and make him feel energetic. With doubt, Du Kang drank a bowl of it. It was really tasty as what the old man said. With fear and courage, Du Kang brought some of the "magical water" to Yellow Emperor who appreciated the flavor of this liquid very much. Instead of blaming, he praised Du Kang and ordered him to make the "magical water" with the excessive grains. At first, the "magical water" was used to sacrifice Heaven and Earth and our ancestors in order to get their blessings. Since then, it has become one of the most important sacrificial offerings. Yellow Emperor ordered Cang Jie, the inventor of Chinese characters, to name this liquid "酒" (jiu).

Later, people found many other functions of wine. Drinking proper amount of wine is beneficial to our health and it can be used to treat diseases as well. It can also make people feel encouraged and in high spirit, thus, soldiers would drink wine before going to the battlefields. Moreover, wine can make people forget worries, as the Chinese saying goes, "Being drunk can disperse sorrows." In ancient times, it was believed that wine had the power of contacting ghosts and gods, so wizards always made themselves drunk in order to communicate with gods. Thus, wine has gradually become one of the favorite drinks of the Chinese, and Du Kang was regarded as the "God of Wine".

The Jiahu site in Wuyang County of Henan Province belongs to Peiligang Culture, where some pieces of pottery were discovered. After testing, Professor Patrick Mark Gauvain in University of Pennsylvania came to the conclusion that the residues on those potteries may be sediment of wine or something like that. This discovery proved that wine making in China began as early as 8,000 years ago.

IX. Houyi Shooting Down the Suns to Help People Combat Droughts

If Yu the Great's river-harnessing is a reflection of the remarkable achievements of our ancestors in controlling flood, Houyi's shooting down the

往要饮壮行酒。酒还能让人忘却烦恼，所谓"一醉解千愁"。古时，人们还认为酒能"交接神鬼"，因而巫师常常以醉酒作为通神的手段。就这样，酒逐渐成为中国人最喜爱的饮品之一，而最早酿酒的杜康也被后人奉为"酒神"。

河南舞阳贾湖遗址属于距今8 000年的裴李岗文化，那里出土的一个陶片上还留有些许残留物。美国宾夕法尼亚大学教授帕特里·马克·高文（Patrick Mark Gauvain）经过化验分析，发现残留物是酒类饮料的沉淀物，这一发现说明中国8 000年前就开始酿酒了。

九、后羿射日助人抗旱

如果说大禹治水反映了先民防治水患的成就，那么，后羿射日则折射出先民对抗旱灾的努力。因为干旱自古以来就是中原地区的人们经常不得不面对的难题，能否成功抗旱对于农业生产至关重要。

传说尧帝时期，天帝有10个太阳儿子。天帝让他们轮流值日，每天由一个太阳给人间带去光明和温暖。可是这10个太阳对轮流值日感到厌倦了，所以私下商量好一起出来玩。当10个太阳同时出现在天空时，大地上顿时热浪滚滚，土地龟裂，草木生烟，庄稼焦枯，民无所食。尧帝央求女巫为大家求雨，可是女巫很快就被晒得全身脱水。尧帝无奈，只好自己向天帝祷告。于是天帝派擅长射箭的天神羿和妻子嫦娥到人间，想办法帮助尧帝教训天帝那10个调皮的儿子。临行前天帝赐给羿一张红色的神弓和一些白色的神箭。

羿到了人间，取弓搭箭，引而不发，他本想吓一吓10个太阳，把他们赶回家，帮人间解决了问题就算了。可是这10个太阳仗着是天帝的儿子，根本不把羿放在眼里。为了人间千万百姓，羿不再犹豫，他瞄准放箭，向着离他最近的一个太阳射去，只见那个太阳放射出血红色的光芒，然后就从天空滑落下去。羿一口气射落了9个太阳。剩下最后一个

suns shows that ancient people have made great efforts in combating drought. Since ancient times, drought has been a problem people in the Central Plains have to face. Hence, whether they could succeed in combating drought is crucial for agricultural production.

During the reign of Emperor Yao, it was said that there were ten suns whose father was the Emperor of Heaven. To obey their father's order, the ten sons took turns to bring light and warmth to the world, each sun being on duty for one day, whereas they privately talked about hanging out together due to their tiredness of this mission. However, when ten suns appeared in the sky at the same time, a heat wave immediately rolled on the earth, causing terrible consequences including cracked lands, scorched grass and trees, withered crops and widespread famine. Emperor Yao had to beg a witch to pray for rain, but the witch soon suffered from severe dehydration in the sun and was dried into an appalling figure. Faced with such a predicament, Emperor Yao had no choice but to pray to the Emperor of Heaven in person. Knowing that, the Emperor of Heaven dispatched Houyi, god of archery, together with his wife Chang'e to the earth to help Emperor Yao discipline the ten mischievous sons. In addition, he granted Houyi a red bow and some white arrows before their departure.

After descending to the earth, Houyi planned to scare the ten suns away so as to help solve the problems on earth without the intention of really shooting them. These ten suns, however, completely ignored Houyi by virtue of the fact that they were sons of the Emperor of Heaven. For the sake of the people on earth, Houyi shot at the nearest sun without any hesitation so that the sun began to drop from the sky after emitting beams of blood-red light. After shooting down 9 of 10 suns in this way, he was timely prevented from shooting at the last sun by Emperor Yao who said that the whole world would be engulfed in the dark and cold without a sun.

For this reason, Houyi left the last sun alive. The scared sun became well-behaved, rising in the east and setting in the west every day. He no longer dared to act recklessly although he felt tired on duty alone. Since then, such terrible drought has never been seen on earth.

Although eradicating the harm for all the people, Houyi could never return to the Heaven and had to stay in the world with his wife Chang'e since he provoked

太阳时，羿又抽出了一支箭，尧帝及时阻止了他："留下他，不然大地会陷于永远的黑暗和寒冷。"

羿留下了最后一个太阳。这个太阳被吓破了胆，从此规规矩矩，每天从东边升起，从西边落下，尽管一个人值日有些劳累，却再也不敢放肆乱来，从此天下再也没有出现过如此严重的旱灾。

虽然为民除了害，但因为射杀了天帝的9个儿子，使得天帝大怒，后羿因而无法再回到天庭，只能和妻子嫦娥留在人间。尧帝感念他的功劳，将后羿封于商丘。商丘市有个湖，人们为了纪念后羿和他的妻子嫦娥，将其命名为日月湖，日代表后羿射日，月代表嫦娥奔月。

the Emperor of Heaven for shooting his nine sons dead. For his contributions, Emperor Yao claimed Shangqiu as Houyi's feudatory. There is a lake named Sun & Moon Lake in Shangqiu City which is a place where people commemorate the magnificent feat of Houyi and Chang'e. The Sun stands for Houyi shooting down the suns and the Moon for Chang'e flying to the moon.

第五章

农业习俗——诗化的农耕文明

Chapter V

Agricultural Customs

河南地区凭借其得天独厚的自然地理条件孕育了农耕文化并成为中华民族的大粮仓。直至今日，农耕文化依旧深深地影响着这片热土，实实在在的庄稼人也一直传承着这种文化，最鲜明、最直接的表现就是生活习俗和人们日常交流时随口道来的民间谚语。

鉴于习俗的内容太过丰富，远非短短数千字可以涵盖，因此，这里仅以与农业相关的节庆习俗作为切入点，向读者展示河南地区一些独特的农业风俗习惯。

一、立春日，打耕牛

立春是二十四节气的第一个，意味着春天到来，万物复苏，农民要为春耕做准备了。这一天河南民间一般会举行各种迎春活动，其中最独

民间年画《天地长春》，该图展现了立春日打春牛、吃春饼的习俗
Chinese folk New Year painting *Everlasting Spring*
The picture shows the folk custom of beating the spring cattle and eating the spring cake on the day of Beginning of Spring

Henan, with its unique natural geographical conditions, has nurtured splendid farming culture and has become a large granary of the Chinese nation. Until today, this farming culture still has a deep influence on this land. The down-to-earth farmers have been inheriting this culture, of which the most distinct and direct manifestations are reflected in the folk customs and proverbs that comes with people in their daily communication.

Since the customs are so rich in content, far from being covered by just a few thousand words, this chapter only takes the festival customs related to agriculture as the entry point to show readers some unique agricultural customs and habits in Henan.

I. Beginning of Spring

Beginning of Spring refers to the first of the twenty-four solar terms, which means the beginning of the springtime when everything comes back to life. It is the time for the farmers to prepare for the spring ploughing. On this day, generally various folk events are held in Henan to welcome the coming of the spring season, the most unique of which is whipping the ploughing cattle. People make "spring cattle" with colored paper and put dried fruits, like peanuts, walnuts, and dates inside the belly of the paper cattle. On the day of Beginning of Spring, everyone takes the colored whips, of red and green, to slash the "spring cattle" with force. When the belly of the "spring cattle" is broken, everyone would scramble to grab and eat the dried fruits inside the belly. It is said that eating the dried fruits would make the old live longer, the children cleverer, and the young stronger.

II. Eryueer Festival (Longtaitou Festival)

Eryueer, the second day of the second month in the Chinese lunar calendar, is a traditional festival of the Han nationality. It is believed by the folk people to be a day on which the dragons wake up from the dormancy, raise their heads, and rise to the sky, so it is called "Longtaitou Festival" ("Dragons' Raising Heads Festival") or the "Green Dragon Festival". Various events are held on this day, like praying for blessing, disaster elimination, and detoxification.

特的要数打耕牛。人们用彩纸扎成牛的形状，即"春牛"，并在纸牛的肚子里装上花生、核桃、枣等干果，在立春日大家手拿红绿彩鞭，用力抽打"春牛"。等到春牛肚子被打开时，大家便争吃里面的干果，据说老人吃了增寿，孩子吃了增智，年轻人吃了更健壮。

二、二月二，龙抬头

农历二月初二，是汉族的传统节日。民间认为，这一天是龙从蛰伏中醒来，抬头登天的日子，故称"龙抬头节"或"青龙节"。人们会在这一天举行各种祈福、消灾、祛毒的活动。

这一天，河南农村的妇女一般都不动剪刀，不做针线活，怕动了剪刀伤龙体。但是，理发师手里的刀和剪却是最忙的，因为人们争相在这一天剃头理发，叫作"剃龙头，洗龙角"，以求大吉大利，也表达了对龙的尊敬。

在这个节日里，有些地方会举行盛大的祭祖活动。还有些地方邻里间会相互赠送五谷瓜果种子，表达美好祝愿，祈祝五谷丰登。有的地方有撒"灰圈儿"的习俗，即把锅底的灰在院子里撒成一个一个同心圆，寓意粮食满仓。

此外，由于从蛰伏中苏醒的不仅有龙，还有蝎子、蜈蚣等毒虫，因此，民间还有驱虫祛毒的活动。

这一天，人们到田野里采野菜，包饺子，摊煎饼，炒黄豆，煎腊肉，蒸枣馍，改善生活成为节日的一项重要内容。在众多的食俗活动中，摊煎饼和炒黄豆的人最多。民间认为，这一天是东海龙王的生日，煎饼是龙王的胎衣。吃煎饼，是为龙王嚼灾，扔煎饼，是为了掩埋龙王的胎衣。

On this day, women in rural Henan generally do not use scissors, nor do they do any needlework, for fear of wounding the body of the dragon with knives or scissors. However, the barbers are exceptions, as they would be the busiest with their knives and scissors on this day, for people would line up to have their hair cut, called "shaving the dragon's head and washing the dragon's horn", wishing to have great luck in the year by showing respect for the dragons.

At this festival, grand ancestor worshiping activities are held in some places, such as the above mentioned ancestor worshiping temple fair at Taihao Tomb in Huaiyang. In some places, the neighbors would give each other seeds of grains and fruits, to express their best wishes for a bumper grain harvest. In some places, there is a custom of "drawing circles by scattering the ash", namely, drawing concentric circles in the yard by scattering the ash from the bottom of pots, with the moral of a barn full of grains.

In addition, since those waking up from the dormancy are not just dragons, but also poisonous insects such as scorpions and centipedes, there are also folk activities of driving off the poisonous insects and detoxification.

On this day, people would participate in a number of activities, with the main theme of improving their lives by eating better, like going to the fields to pick wild potherbs, making dumplings and pancakes, stir-frying soybeans, frying bacon, and making steamed bread with dates on its top. Among the numerous food customs, the most popular ones are making pancakes and eating stir-fried beans. The folks believe that this day is the birthday of the Dragon King of the East China Sea, and the pancake is considered to be the afterbirth of the Dragon King. Eating pancakes is to relieve disasters for the Dragon King and throwing pancakes is to bury the afterbirth of the Dragon King.

III. Sanyuesan Festival (Shangsi Festival)

Sanyuesan refers to the third day of the third month in the Chinese lunar calendar. People would go to the market to buy some flower seeds, vegetable seeds and then sow them, believing that the flowers planted on this day may grow better and the seeds sowed on this day bear more fruits and vegetables. Many people would go to the fields as well to pick newly sprouted shepherd's purse and eat

三、三月三，上巳节

农历三月三这一天，人们会去赶集买些花籽、菜籽等种下去，认为这一天种下的花长得旺，果蔬收成好。许多人还在这一天到地里挖新发芽的荠菜，与鸡蛋一起食用，鲜美可口。当夜幕降临时，家家要燃放鞭炮，驱邪逐鬼，以求平安。

四、五月初五端午节

河南的端午习俗丰富多彩。有民谣这样说："五月五，麦子熟，包好粽子过端午。"这说明包粽子、吃粽子是端午节一项重要的民俗活动。从粽子的形状上说，河南的粽子主要是三角粽和四角粽。端午节时，河南人不仅要吃粽子，还要吃油炸食品。像油条、麻花、麻叶等，都是人们常做的油炸食品。在众多的油炸食品中，糖糕和菜角是最典型最有代表性的节日食品。端午节这天，最兴奋的要数孩子们，他们穿上五毒肚兜，手脚系着五色彩线，脖子上挂着精美的香囊。

五、六月初一过小年

每年的农历六月初一到初六，是中原民间比较重要的节日，俗称"过小年"。这时一年已过半，农民刚收获了小麦，丰收的喜悦洋溢在心头眉梢。同时，秋天的作物也已经播种，在这个中原农耕地区的"收获节"里，人们庆祝丰收、祈求丰年。人们在屋中、院内、麦场摆上供桌，放上馍、枣山（装点有枣的馍）和桃、李等五种瓜果，再摆上新收的小麦，然后焚香，祈求秋季风调雨顺、五谷丰登。然后大家围坐在一起，高高兴兴地吃上一顿用肉、青菜、粉条、海带等做成

together with eggs, which taste delicious. When the night falls, firecrackers would be set off in each household to exorcise the evil spirits for peace.

IV. Dragon Boat Festival

Dragon Boat Festival is observed on the fifth day of the fifth month in the Chinese lunar calendar. The customs in Henan are colorful and rich in variety. As a folk song goes, "The wheat is ripening, on the fifth day of the fifth month, and make Zongzi (rice dumplings), well ready for the Day (Dragon Boat Festival)", which indicates that making and eating rice dumplings are important folk activities during the Dragon Boat Festival in Henan. In terms of shape, rice dumplings are mainly triangular and square shaped in Henan. During the Dragon Boat Festival, people in Henan eat not only rice dumplings, but fried foods as well, among which the ones that people often make include Youtiao (fried dough sticks), Mahua (fried twisty donuts), Maye (fried dough leaves with sesames), etc. Among the numerous fried foods, Tanggao (fried sugar cakes) and Caijiao (fried vegetable pies in half-moon shape) are the most typical and representative festival foods. On the Dragon Boat Festival, children are most excited. They are supposed to wear bellybands against the five poisonous creatures, with five-color threads tied around their wrists and ankles, and beautiful perfume sachets hanging around their necks.

V. The Little Lunar New Year

Commonly known as the "Little Lunar New Year", which lasts from the first day to the sixth day of the sixth month in the Chinese lunar calendar, it is a relatively important folk festival in the Central Plains every year. With over a half of the year gone past, and the wheat having just been harvested, the farmers are overwhelmed with the joy of harvest. Moreover, the autumn crops have already been sown. In this "Harvest Festival" for the farming areas in the Central Plains, people celebrate the harvest and pray for another one in the coming year. They first put altar tables in the house, in the courtyard, or in the wheat threshing ground, on which they lay out foods like steamed buns, date hills (steamed buns decorated with dates), five kinds of fruits and melons, such as peaches and plums,

民间年画《庄稼忙》,该图描绘了夏季麦收时节,农村男女老少在麦场中忙碌收获的喜悦场面

Chinese folk New Year painting *Farmers Busy Harvesting Crops*
The painting depicts the happy scene of rural men, women and children busy harvesting wheat on the threshing floor in the summer wheat harvesting season

的杂烩菜。

在这个节日里,家家户户还要把已出嫁的姑娘接回家,尽心款待后再送回婆家,因此又叫"闺女节"。农村里农活繁忙,女孩子们一旦出嫁,就要终日劳作,很少有机会彻底放松休息,这个节日使已嫁作他人妇的女人不仅能与亲人团聚,还能再体验一下被父母宠爱的美好旧时光。

and the newly harvested wheat, and then they burn the incense, and pray for good weather in the coming autumn and a bumper grain harvest for the year. Finally, they sit around and enjoy a meal of "chowder" of meat, green vegetables, vermicelli, and seaweed, etc.

During this festival, every household is supposed to welcome the married daughter home, and after treating her with great hospitality, would send her back to her mother-in-law's home. So this festival is also called "Daughter's Day". In the rural areas, girls, once married, with a lot of farm work to do, will have to toil all day long. There is no opportunity for them to relax completely. This festival enables married daughters to have a chance to reunite with their family members, and to recapture the good old days, when they was held by the parental affection.

VI. Qixi Festival (Double-Seventh Day)

The 7th day of the 7th month in the Chinese lunar calendar is called the Qiqiao Festival, and the yearly meeting day for the (mythical) Cowherd and the Weaver Maid. This romantic festival is girls' "Begging Day for Dexterity", namely, a day for praying to the Weaver Maid for giving them dexterity, helping them to become ingenious and good at spinning, weaving and embroidery.

The rituals of "begging for dexterity" are usually held in the evening of the day. Girls would place sacrifices of fresh fruits, food and wine in the courtyard or on the terrace. But what comes next varies from place to place in Henan. For example, in some places, the girls would face the moon to thread the needle. Then, with the threaded needle, they closed eyes, and sting the melon flower. Those who succeed in stinging the flower once are considered to be dexterous, and those who succeed in stinging the flower seven times in a row are praised as "weaving girls". In other places, a bag of embroidery needles, as fine as the cow hair, are scattered on the ground in the moonlight for girls to find, and those who can find any of them are considered to be dexterous. Whichever form it is, the core of the tradition is to test a girl's eyesight, patience, and carefulness.

六、七月七，乞巧节

农历七月初七是"七夕节"，是牛郎织女一年一度相会的日子。这样一个浪漫的节日也是少女们的"乞巧节"，祈求织女"送巧"，帮助她们变得心灵手巧，擅长纺线、织布和刺绣。

乞巧的仪式一般在晚上举行，少女们在庭院里或楼台上供上鲜果和酒菜，接下来的活动河南各地不尽相同。比如，在有些地方，少女们一起对月穿针，并拿着穿上线的针，闭上眼睛刺瓜花，能一针刺中的被认为手巧，如果能连续七次刺中，就被赞为"织女"。在有些地

明代《汉宫乞巧图》局部
该图描绘的是七夕晚上中国古代少女在庭院里祭拜织女的场景
Part of the Ming Dynasty painting *The Girls Worshiping the Weaver Maid in the Han Palace*
The painting depicts the scene of ancient Chinese girls worshiping the Weaver Maid in the courtyard on the evening of Qixi Festival

VII. Zhongyuan Festival

The 15th day of the 7th month in the Chinese lunar calendar is the Zhongyuan Festival, also known as the "Ghost Festival". On this day, people would visit the ancestral halls or the ancestral graves to worship the dead by burning incense and paper money. In the evening, street lamps would be set up and lit on for the lonely ghosts, and people living along the river would put lit lanterns in the river, which are commonly known as "lighting up road lamps" and "lighting up the river lanterns". At the same time, incense and paper money are burned to release souls of the dead from suffering.

In the northern part of Henan, the 15th day of the 7th lunar month is also known as the "Working Animals Festival". There are many events to worship the working animals. As the Central Plains is a farming area, large working animals, like the cattle and mules, are the main "laborers" for ploughing. In addition, the past autumn ploughing is the most strenuous labor for the working animals. Therefore, every household would make lamb-shaped steamed bread of white wheat flour, place it on the table for worshiping (the working animals), and then set off firecrackers, praying for the prosperity of the livestock of the household. On this day, working animals, like the ploughing cattle, mules, and horses, are given a day's rest, and meanwhile, are fed with fine fodder to thank them for their contribution to the autumn ploughing. The establishment of the "Working Animals Festival" shows, as one can see, the great importance that people attach to livestock, the importance of livestock in agricultural production, and the harmonious relationship between human and the livestock.

VIII. Laba Festival

Laba Festival falls on the 8th day of the 12th month in the Chinese lunar calendar. People of each household are supposed to have laba porridge for a meal on this day. Laba porridge is made from various grains, beans and dried fruits that have been just harvested in the very year. It is generally sweet, but salty in some places. To make salty porridge, turnips, cabbage, vermicelli, kelp and tofu are added to the conventional ingredients, like rice, millet, mung beans, cowpea,

方，人们把一包细如牛毛的绣花针撒在月亮照亮的地上，能摸到绣花针的人为巧。无论何种形式，考验的都是女孩子们的眼力、耐心和细心程度。

七、七月十五中元节

农历七月十五是中元节，又称"鬼节"。这一天，人们白天要祭先祠、上祖坟，燃香烧纸，祭奠死者，晚上还要为孤魂野鬼设路灯。沿河居住的人家则要在河里燃灯，俗称"放路灯""放河灯"，同时焚香烧纸，以超度亡灵。

在河南北部地区，农历七月十五还被称为"牲口节"，有许多敬奉耕牛的活动。中原是农耕地区，牛、骡子等牲口是耕地的主要"劳力"，刚过去的秋耕又是牲口最繁重的劳动。因此，家家都要蒸羊羔形状的白面馍，供奉在案桌上，然后燃放鞭炮，祈愿家中牲畜兴旺。这一天，有耕牛、骡马的人家都要让牲口休息一天，同时给牲口喂精饲料，以感谢它们在秋耕中做出的贡献。"牲口节"的设立足见人们对牲畜的重视，体现了牲畜在农业生产中的重要性，以及人畜间的和谐关系。

八、十二月初八腊八节

每年农历十二月初八是腊八节，这一天家家户户都要喝腊八粥。腊八粥用当年新收获的各种谷物、豆类和干果熬制而成，一般是甜的，也有的地方做成咸的。咸的腊八粥除了用常规的大米、小米、绿豆、豇豆、花生、大枣等原料外，还加入了萝卜、白菜、粉条、海带和豆腐等。

对河南人来说，腊八是春节的序幕，有句俗话，"吃了腊八粥，就

peanuts, and dates.

For Henan people, Laba Festival is the prelude to the Spring Festival, as the saying goes, "After having had laba porridge it's time to stock up for Spring Festival." That is to say, after the Laba Festival, it's time for people to prepare for the Spring Festival, the most important festival of a year.

IX. Agricultural Proverbs

Agricultural proverbs are the summary of farmers' experience in agricultural production. There are numerous agricultural proverbs in Henan. Simple and concise in language, catchy, and easy to remember, for thousands of years these proverbs have been passed down from generation to generation by farmers in the Central Plains. These proverbs, covering almost all aspects of agricultural production, some teaching farming methods, some reminding farmers of the farming time, some connected with weather forecast, and so on, have been guiding people through their practical production activities for thousands of years. The twenty-four solar terms in China were originally created for agricultural production. Each solar term is concerned with some corresponding agricultural activities, and therefore related to a number of agricultural proverbs. The following are the introductions of some commonly used agricultural proverbs, with solar terms as the clues, to get a glimpse into the essence of agricultural proverbs in the Central Plains.

The Beginning of Spring, generally around February 4 in the Gregorian calendar, is the first of the twenty-four solar terms, which marks the beginning of the spring season. At this time, with the gradual rising of the temperature in Henan, the land begins to thaw, and everything begins to germinate, so an agricultural proverb goes like "Three days after the Beginning of Spring, all kinds of grass will be sprouting". With the ceremony of beating the ploughing cattle, namely, the aforementioned beating of the spring cattle made of paper with colored whips, people start the agricultural activities of the year. Since the Beginning of Spring coincides with the beginning of the sixth nine-day cold period, there goes the agricultural proverb "The whipping of the spring cattle marks the beginning of the sixth nine-day cold period, with spring cattle seen

把年来办",意思是过了腊八,人们就该为春节这个最隆重的节日做准备了。

九、农谚

农谚是人们对农业生产经验的总结。河南农谚数量众多,语言简单精练、朗朗上口、易于记诵,千百年来为中原农民代代相传,有的教导耕种方法,有的提醒耕种时间,有的关乎天气预测……总之,农谚涵盖了农业生产的方方面面,指导着人们的实践活动。中国的二十四节气本就是围绕农业生产而创制的,每个节气都有对应的农事活动,自然也有不少相关的农谚,下面以节气为线索介绍一些常用的农谚,使大家以此管窥中原农谚的精髓。

立春一般在公历2月4日前后,是二十四节气之首,代表春天的开始。这时,河南地区气温逐渐上升,大地解冻,万物复苏,因此有"立春三日,百草发芽"的农谚。人们用"打春"仪式,即前述用彩鞭鞭打纸做的春牛,来开启一年的农事活动。由于立春恰逢"六九"的开头,因此又有"春打六九头,遍地是耕牛"的农谚。

雨水一般在公历2月19日前后,河南大部分地区雨量逐渐增加,适合农作物生长,对应的农谚有"雨水有雨庄稼好,大春小春一片宝"。

惊蛰在公历3月6日前后,天气转暖,春雷初响,冬眠的动物纷纷苏醒,出土活动,意味着紧张的春耕大忙要到了,因此有农谚"过了惊蛰节,春耕不能歇",以及"惊蛰不耙地,好像蒸馍跑了气",意思是在这个耕作的关键时候,如果不好好干,开个好头,以后再努力也会事倍功半。

春分一般在公历3月21日前后。从惊蛰开始,农活一日更比一日忙。春分时,昼夜长短相等,是最适合麦苗生长的时节,有"春分麦起身,一刻值千金",以及"麦过春分昼夜忙"的农谚,农民们不仅要昼

everywhere in the field".

Rain Water is around February 19 in the Gregorian calendar, when rainfall increases gradually in most parts of Henan, which is suitable for growth of crops. The corresponding agricultural proverb goes like "Rainfalls around Rain Water, surely will bring crops laughter, sown or harvested in spring, each will be a treasured thing".

The Waking of Insects falls around March 6 in the Gregorian calendar, when it gets warm, the spring thunder breaks out, and awakened hibernating animals begin to come out of their dens one after another to move about. This means that the intense and busy spring ploughing is coming, so there is one agricultural proverb going like "After Waking of Insects, a farmer never rests, when the spring ploughing presses", and another going like "After the Waking of Insects, if a farmer does not rake his land, it is like steamed-bread making with steam leaking". Both proverbs mean, at this critical moment of spring ploughing, without working hard to make a good beginning, a farmer, however hard he may try later, will get only half the result with twice the effort.

The Vernal Equinox is around March 21st. Since the Waking of Insects, farmers begin to get busier and busier day by day. When the Vernal Equinox arrives, with day and night equal in length, it is the most suitable time for the growth of wheat in Henan. There are agricultural proverbs going like "Around the Vernal Equinox, when the wheat starts to sprout, even a moment counts", and "After Vernal Equinox, with wheat, farmers get busy night and day". Farmers have to work day and night in the field, on the other hand, they have to take good care of the livestock, lest they graze on the wheat seedlings.

After Qingming Festival (Tomb-Sweeping Day, around April 5 of the Gregorian calendar), the weather is fine, the climate is warm, and farmers get even busier with the farming in spring. The solar term that comes next is the Grain Rain, which falls around April 20th in the Gregorian calendar. With rainfalls increasing, and the weather getting warmer, the crops are growing vigorously. This is a good time to plant cotton. If you miss the time, as the agricultural proverb goes, "Plant cotton around the Beginning of Summer, and you will get in nothing but seedlings", meaning that if cotton is planted late, till after the Beginning of Summer, it will grow only in stems and stalks but will not bear cotton bolls.

夜在地里劳作，还要看好牲畜，免得它们啃食麦苗。

清明节（一般在公历4月5日左右）后，天气晴朗，气候温暖，春耕更加繁忙。接下来是公历4月20日前后的谷雨，雨水增多，天气暖和，作物生长旺盛，此时是种棉花的大好时节，如果错过了，就如农谚所说的，"立夏种棉花，有苗没疙瘩"，意思是过了立夏再种棉花，棉花就只长枝干，不结棉桃了。谷雨时小麦开始抽穗，"一穗二穗，四十天上囤"，意思是从谷雨算起，再有40天小麦就能成熟收割了。

立夏一般在公历5月6日前后，意味着春季结束，夏季开始。这时，随着作物的生长，杂草长得也越来越旺，和作物争肥，需要进行中耕除草，农谚有"立夏三朝遍地锄"。这时小麦已经出齐麦穗，开始扬花上浆，很快就要成熟了，需要提前做好收割的准备，包括把打麦用的场地碾压平实，否则"立夏不碾场，麦在土里扬"，影响最后的收成。

小满一般在公历5月21日前后。这时节，麦子很快就要成熟了，"立夏麦穗齐，小满硬了仁"，"小满十八天，麦不熟也青干"。前一句指小满时麦子已灌足了浆，变得饱满了，后一句指小满后约18天就是收割的时间了。小满还是种芝麻和谷子的时节，农谚有"小满种芝麻，节节都开花"，以及"小满种谷，打满仓屋"等。

芒种一般在公历6月6日前后。此时河南各地天气开始热起来，小麦进入收割期，同时还需抢种秋季作物，因此农事异常繁忙，谚语"火麦连天"描述了农民热火朝天收麦的场景。

夏至一般在公历6月22日前后，这时白昼最长，气温持续升高，夏熟作物如棉花等长势旺盛，需要进行中耕除草，农谚云"夏至棉田草，胜似毒蛇咬"。

小暑一般在公历7月7日前后，预示着河南大部分地区开始进入一年中最热的时节，需要播种秋熟作物，急需雨水的滋润，农谚"小暑一滴

Around the time of Grain Rain, wheat begins to head, as the saying goes, "One ear or two ears, forty days in barns", meaning that from the time of the Grain Rain, wheat will be ripe for harvesting in 40 days.

The Beginning of Summer is around May 6th in the Gregorian calendar, meaning the end of spring and the beginning of summer. At this time, as the crops grow, the weeds grow more and more vigorously as well, competing with the crops for fertilizer, making intertillage weeding operations necessary, as an agricultural proverb goes, "Three days after the Beginning of Summer, hoeing is needed everywhere". At this time, the wheat, having all grown out of the heading stage, has now got into the flowering and filling stages, and will soon be ripe. Preparations, like making the wheat threshing floor compact and even by crushing and rolling, should be made in advance for harvesting. Otherwise, the eventual harvest will be affected, as the proverb goes, "If the wheat threshing floor is not made ready around the Beginning of Summer, the wheat grains will have to be winnowed with the soil".

The Grain Full is around May 21 in the Gregorian calendar. At this time, the wheat will soon be ripe, as proverbs go, "Around the Beginning of Summer, the wheat crops have all got their ears, and around the Grain Full, the hardness of kernels has gained", "18 days after the Grain Full, green wheat is dry, even if it is not ripe". The former means that around the Grain Full, the kernels, having been filled with enough pulp, are getting plumper, and the later means that about 18 days after the Grain Full, it will be time for harvesting the wheat. Grain Full is also the season for growing sesame and millet. As the agricultural proverbs go, "Grow sesame around the Grain Full, it will put forth blossoms notch by notch", "Grow millet around the Grain Full, barns will be filled with harvest gains".

The Grain in Ear falls around June 6 in the Gregorian calendar. At this time, it's getting hot throughout Henan, with wheat in the harvesting period. And it is also time for rush-planting autumn crops. Therefore, people are getting extremely busy with farm work, and there goes the proverb "Harvesting wheat in successive heat", describing the scene of farmers rushing to harvest wheat.

The Summer Solstice is around June 22 in the Gregorian calendar. At this time, the daytime is the longest, the temperature continues to rise, and the summer crops such as cotton are growing vigorously, making intertillage weeding

雨，遍地是黄金"道出了这个时节雨水的珍贵。

大暑一般在公历7月23日前后，是一年里最为炎热干燥的时候。这时夏熟作物生长迅速，消耗大量水分，有时需要人工浇灌，以弥补雨水的不足，否则影响收成，因此有农谚"大暑不浇苗，到老无好稻"。

进入8月份，暑热渐退，8月8日左右是立秋，即秋季的开始，白天气温尚高，但早晚气温较低，农谚云"立罢秋，早上晚上凉飕飕"。到8月23日左右为处暑，"处"是终止的意思，表示暑气逐渐消失，气温下降，雨量减少。农谚"处暑提镰割早稻"描述了农民忙于收割早稻的情况。

9月8日前后的节气是白露，这个时期，由于夜里温度低，早上地面会出现凝结的白色露珠。此时大部分地区天气渐凉，"过了白露节，夜寒白日热"。秋季作物进入成熟期，开始收获高粱，"白露提镰不论青"。9月23日前后的节气是秋分，此时河南大部分地区的农民忙于秋收和秋种，此时，如果下场秋雨，有利于农作物的生长，农谚有"秋分有雨来年丰"。

从寒露到霜降，即大约每年的10月8日到23日，天气逐渐转冷，露珠凝结成了白霜。这15天也是秋收最忙的时候，农民既要抢收豆类作物，还要抢种过冬麦类作物。"寒露至霜降，种麦莫商量"，"秋分早，霜降迟，寒露种麦正当时"，"寒露豆霜降麦，种了小麦种大麦"，这几个农谚都道出了农民忙完收豆忙种麦的情景。这种忙碌一直要持续到立冬，即11月7日前后，"霜降到立冬，种麦莫放松"。

立冬意味着黄河中下游地区开始进入冬季。这时，作物都已收割，过冬的小麦也已播种，农忙基本结束。当然，农忙结束不等于农民可以完全放松休息了，从立冬到小雪（11月22日前后）、大雪（12月7日前后）、冬至（12月22日前后），再到小寒（1月7日前后），这两个月里，农民还需要进行冬耕，给土壤增肥，为来年的农业生产打好基础。"立了冬，把地耕，能使土里养分增"，"大雪冬至雪花飞，搞好副业

operations necessary, as the agricultural proverb goes, "Around the Summer Solstice the cotton field weed is more harmful than the bite of a venomous snake".

The Slight Heat is around July 7 in the Gregorian calendar each year, indicating that most parts of Henan begin to enter the hottest season of the year. As it's time to sow the autumn crops, rain water is in great need to moisten the fields, as the agricultural proverb puts it, "Around the Slight Heat a drop of rain falls, scatters gold everywhere", indicating how precious the rain water is in this season.

The Great Heat is around July 23 of each year in the Gregorian calendar. As it is the hottest and the driest time of the year, summer crops grow so rapidly and consume so much water at this time that it is necessary to water the crops artificially from time to time due to the shortage of rainwater, otherwise, harvest will be affected. So an agricultural proverb goes, "Around the Great Heat, water the rice seedlings, or you will never have a good harvest".

In August, the summer heat is gradually receding. And around August 8, the Beginning of Autumn falls, meaning the start of autumn. The temperature is still high during the day while relatively low in the morning and evening. As an agricultural proverb puts it, "Right after the Beginning of Autumn, it gets cool, in both the morning and the evening". And around August 23, falls the Limit of Heat. The Chinese character for the Limit of Heat is "Chu Shu", in which the character "Chu" means ending, indicating that the summer heat is gradually disappearing, the temperature is falling, and the rainfall is decreasing. The agricultural proverb "Around the Limit of Heat, it's time to lift the sickle and reap the early rice" describes the situation in which farmers are busy harvesting their early rice.

The solar term around September 8 is the White Dew. During this period of time, due to the low temperature at night, white drops of dew of condensed moisture will appear on the ground in the morning. The weather in most areas is gradually getting cooler, as is described by the saying "After the White Dew, it gets chilly at night yet still hot during the day". Autumn crops are ripening, and sorghum comes first for harvesting, as goes the saying, "Around White Dew, lift your sickle, regardless of the green color of the crops". Around September 23 falls the solar term Autumnal Equinox. Farmers in most parts of Henan are busy with autumn harvesting and planting. And an autumn rain at this time is good for the growth of crops, as the agricultural saying puts it, "If it is raining around the

多积肥"。

小寒（1月7日前后）到大寒（1月20日前后）是一年中最冷的时候，"大寒小寒，杀猪过年"，忙碌了一年的农民终于可以放松下来，开始置备年货，准备庆祝全年最隆重的节日——春节。

Autumnal Equinox, a good harvest is coming for the year following".

From the Cold Dew to the Frost's Descent, that is, from around October 8 to 23 each year, the weather gradually turns cold and the dewdrops begin to be coagulated into hoarfrost. These 15 days are also the busiest time for the autumn harvest. Farmers have to rush-harvest the bean crops, and to rush-plant the winter grain crops right afterwards. Agricultural proverbs like "From the Cold Dew to the Frost's Descent, it's time for sowing wheat, with no need to ask for anyone's consent", "With the Autumnal Equinox too early, and the Frost's Descent too late, the Cold Dew comes just in time for sowing wheat", and "Cold Dew is time for harvesting beans, and Frost's Descent time for sowing grains, with wheat and barley sowed in turns", have all described the situations of farmers' busy work of getting in the bean crops and sowing the grain crops. This busy period usually lasts until the Beginning of Winter, that is, around November 7, as is described in the saying "From the Frost's Descent to the Beginning of Winter, there is no relaxation for wheat sowing".

The Beginning of Winter means that winter has arrived around the middle and lower reaches of the Yellow River. With crops having been harvested and winter wheat having been sowed, the busy farming has basically come to an end. Of course, the end of busy farming does not mean that farmers can completely relax. In the two months starting from the Beginning of Winter to Slight Snow (around November 22), to Great Snow (around December 7), to Winter Solstice (around December 22), and then to Slight Cold (January 7), farmers still need to carry out winter ploughing to increase soil fertility and to lay the foundation for agricultural production in the coming year. As the sayings put, "Around the Beginning of Winter, till the soil to increase its fertility", "Around the Great Snow and the Winter Solstice when snowflakes are flying, do well in the sidelines and in manure collecting".

From the Slight Cold (around January 7) to the Great Cold (around January 20), it is the coldest time of the year. "Between the Slight Cold and Great Cold, it's time to slaughter pigs for the Spring Festival." The farmers, having been busy for a whole year, eventually have time to relax themselves, start to prepare goods for the coming new year, and get ready to celebrate the most important festival of the year—the Spring Festival.

附录
Appendix

中国历史年代简表
A Brief Chronology of Chinese History

五帝时代 Period of the Five Legendary Rulers c. 2600 BC-c. 2070 BC	黄帝 Huangdi (Yellow Emperor)	
	颛顼 Zhuanxu	
	帝喾 Diku (Emperor Ku)	
	尧 Yao	
	舜 Shun	
夏 Xia Dynasty	c. 2070 BC- c. 1600 BC	
商 Shang Dynasty	c. 1600 BC- c. 1046 BC	
西周 Western Zhou Dynasty	c. 1046 BC- c. 771 BC	
东周 Eastern Zhou Dynasty 770 BC-256 BC	春秋 Spring and Autumn Period	770 BC-476 BC
	战国 Warring States Period	475 BC-221 BC
秦 Qin Dynasty	221 BC-206 BC	
汉 Han Dynasty 206 BC-220 AD	西汉 Western Han	206 BC-25 AD
	东汉 Eastern Han	25 AD-220 AD
三国 Three Kingdoms 220 AD-280 AD	魏 Wei	220 AD-265 AD
	蜀汉 Shu Han	221 AD-263 AD
	吴 Wu	222 AD-280 AD
晋 Jin Dynasty 265 AD–420 AD	西晋 Western Jin	265 AD-317 AD
	东晋 Eastern Jin	317 AD-420 AD

Appendix

续表 Continued Table

南北朝 Southern and Northern Dynasties 420 AD-589 AD	南朝 Southern Dynasties	宋 Song	420 AD-479 AD
		齐 Qi	479 AD-502 AD
		梁 Liang	502 AD-557 AD
		陈 Chen	557 AD-589 AD
	北朝 Northern Dynasties	北魏 Northern Wei	386 AD-534 AD
		东魏 Eastern Wei	534 AD-550 AD
		北齐 Northern Qi	550 AD-577 AD
		西魏 Western Wei	535 AD-556 AD
		北周 Northern Zhou	557 AD-581 AD
隋 Sui Dynasty			581 AD-618 AD
唐 Tang Dynasty			618 AD-907 AD
五代十国 Five Dynasties and Ten States	五代 Five Dynasties 907 AD-960 AD	后梁 Later Liang	907 AD-923 AD
		后唐 Later Tang	923 AD-936 AD
		后晋 Later Jin	936 AD-947 AD
		后汉 Later Han	947 AD-950 AD
		后周 Later Zhou	951 AD-960 AD
	十国 Ten States 902 AD-979 AD	北汉 Northern Han	951 AD-979 AD
		吴 Wu	902 AD-937 AD
		吴越 Wuyue	907 AD-978 AD
		闽 Min	909 AD-945 AD
		南汉 Southern Han	917 AD-971 AD
		荆南(又称"南平") Jingnan (Nanping)	924 AD-963 AD
		楚 Chu	927 AD-951 AD
		南唐 Southern Tang	937 AD-975 AD
		前蜀 Former Shu	907 AD-925 AD
		后蜀 Later Shu	934 AD-965 AD

续表 Continued Table

宋 Song Dynasty 960 AD-1279 AD	北宋 Northern Song	960 AD-1127 AD
	南宋 Southern Song	1127 AD-1279 AD
辽 Liao (契丹 Qidan/Khitan)	907 AD-1125 AD	
金 Jin	1115 AD-1234 AD	
西夏 Xixia (Tangut)	1038 AD-1227 AD	
元 Yuan Dynasty	1206 AD-1368 AD	
明 Ming Dynasty	1368 AD-1644 AD	
清 Qing Dynasty	1616 AD-1911 AD	
中华民国 Republic of China	1912 AD-1949 AD	
中华人民共和国 People's Republic of China	1949 AD-